MY DARLING LEMON THYME

MY DARLING LEMON THYME

Recipes from my real food kitchen

Emma Galloway

ROOST
BOOKS

Boston · 2015

Roost Books
An imprint of Shambhala Publications, Inc.
Horticultural Hall
300 Massachusetts Avenue
Boston, Massachusetts 02115
roostbooks.com

First published in 2014 by HarperCollins Publishers (New Zealand) Limited
Unit D1, 63 Apollo Drive, Rosedale, Auckland 0632, New Zealand
harpercollins.co.nz

9 8 7 6 5 4 3 2 1
All photographs by Emma Galloway, with the following exceptions:
p. 8 and back cover: Louie Galloway
p. 92 (chopping chocolate): DeArna Stanley-Joblin
p. 92 (handheld beater): Priscilla Spooner
Line drawings by Ada Nguyen
Cover and interior design: Anna Egan-Reid

First U.S. Edition
Printed in China

⊗ This edition is printed on acid-free paper that meets the
American National Standards Institute Z39.48 Standard.
♻ Shambhala Publications makes every effort to print on recycled paper.
For more information please visit www.shambhala.com.
Distributed in the United States by Penguin Random House LLC
and in Canada by Random House of Canada Ltd

Library of Congress Cataloging-in-Publication Data
Galloway, Emma.
My darling lemon thyme: recipes from my real food kitchen /
Emma Galloway.—First U.S. edition.
pages   cm
Includes index.
Originally published: Auckland: HarperCollins Publishers, 2014.
ISBN 978-1-61180-270-2 (pbk.: acid-free paper)
1. Vegetarian cooking. 2. Cooking, Australian. 3. Cooking, New Zealand. I. Title.
TX837.G287 2015
641.5'636—dc23
2015009236

CONTENTS

INTRODUCTION 7
PANTRY INGREDIENTS 11

RISE + SHINE 27
SMALL PLATES 61
SWEET TOOTH 93
BIG PLATES 125
DRINKS + FROZEN GOODNESS 161
SWEETNESS 191
ETC. 219

MUCH LOVE . . . 245
INDEX 249

INTRODUCTION

I grew up in the tiny surf town of Raglan on the west coast of the North Island of New Zealand. At a time when many families were buying their first microwave oven and tucking into ready-made meals, we were living an altogether different life.

Our family of seven (I have two brothers and two sisters) lived in a wooden house built by my father—its stained-glass windows greeted anyone who approached the front door. Drinking water came straight from the sky and into our tank, fruit and vegetables were grown in the traditional way, and we collected raw goat's milk from a farm at the end of our winding gravel road, both to drink and make yogurt. Looking back, it seems like a fairy tale, but it's exactly the life I now want to give my own two children.

Food was a central part of our daily life. As vegetarians, we paid a lot of attention to what we ate, ensuring the right combinations of foods were eaten together to maximize the nutritional benefits. Eating seasonally was a way of life, not just a catchphrase. Dried kelp and nutritional yeast were sprinkled onto everything, brown rice was the only rice we knew, and banana cake was always made using whole-wheat flour and topped off with frosting flavored with carob, never cocoa. I don't ever remember feeling that we were missing out by not eating meat, undoubtedly because of the love and time my mother put into preparing our amazing meals. I've tried to continue this for my own little family: we celebrate what we can eat and don't worry too much about what we can't. Mum's life revolved around the well-being of her children, whether it was helping Dad grow the vegetables that fed us, nourishing us with her homemade food, or reading up on natural remedies if we were ill.

I can only imagine how tough it must have been for my parents to go against the grain and bring up their children in an alternative way. Thankfully times have changed and nowadays being vegetarian or choosing to tread lightly on this earth is not frowned upon—quite the opposite, it's all the rage!

Other than a fleeting moment when I considered going to art school, being a chef is the only thing I've ever wanted to be. My first job, when I'd just turned 17 and was in my final year of high school, only sparked my determination to pursue my dream. The silence of the early-morning kitchen, the smell of coffee in the air, and that first batch of muffins coming out of the oven are still memories that bring a smile to my face. And the energy of the kitchen during night shift, with the music cranking and conversation flowing, always left me exhausted and yet so full of energy and ideas that I found it hard to switch off when I finally hit the pillow.

After a year of cooking nights and weekends, I'd truly gotten the restaurant bug. I went on to train as a chef before moving to Sydney, where I worked in the pastry sections of two of the city's top catering companies and fell in love with all things sweet. And, in the beautiful beach town of Byron Bay, I met a cute Australian-raised Vietnamese boy who stole my heart.

After eight years of cooking professionally I gave it up to become a mum. I'd be lying if I said it's been an easy ride. Our daughter, Ada, came into this world kicking and screaming and then didn't stop for the first year of her life. It was suggested by my midwife that I cut out gluten and dairy. I did (but only halfheartedly, given that I knew nothing about allergy-free living at the time), and a little bit of normality came creeping back into our lives. During my second pregnancy I went back to eating whatever I wanted, only to suffer pain in my gut and more headaches than normal. I attributed it to pregnancy and along came our son, Kye, kicking and screaming just as much as his sister had done, and quickly developing a thick crust of eczema on his scalp. It took just a few weeks for me to get serious this time. The whole family was allergy-tested and we cut all gluten, dairy, and cane sugar out of our diet for over two years. It was tough—as any mum knows, in those early days you often just try to eat whatever you can grab. There were many moments when it all felt too hard; when I felt I couldn't eat anything at all. But slowly, slowly this new way of eating became easy and I've never looked back.

Having eaten a predominantly whole-food diet before we began, it was a shock to me to see how little was on offer to those with allergies. Every product on the market and every recipe I came across made a poor substitute, nutrition-ally, for what we had previously been eating, and most tasted about as good as cardboard. So, rather than go down the gluten-free route of pre-packaged nutrition-free, gluten-free flour mixes and overpriced packaged foods, I was drawn down the whole-food, made-from-scratch path. Now that the kids are school age and not nearly as sensitive as they once were, I have introduced a little dairy back into our diets, but we still don't do too well with gluten.

So yes, we do live meat-free and gluten-free, we do avoid most dairy, and I prefer to use unrefined sweeteners but, above all, we just eat *real* food. That's food as it's supposed to be, whole and unadulterated, fresh from the earth, prepared with minimal fuss, and eaten in a way that nourishes our bodies. We eat real food my grandparents would recognize, not the food-like products humankind has developed to make our lives easier but which in reality seem to make us ever more unhealthy.

My own personal belief is that everyone can benefit from eating less wheat, meat, and dairy in their diet. If not completely, then at least most of the time. But my recipes aren't just for those with food intolerances or allergies or for those who choose to eat meat-free. They're for everyone who wants to enjoy a better life and celebrate nutritious, wholesome, *real* cooking. This is, in my small way, an attempt to show people another way of eating, of living, and of being.

PANTRY INGREDIENTS

Bypass the ready-made, overpriced, nutritionless, processed foods on many supermarket shelves and take charge of what you put into your mouth. Here's a guide to all the good stuff that fills my pantry and fridge and provides the starting point for most of the recipes in this book.

flours

At any one time I keep well over 15 different gluten-free flours on hand, but for the purpose of this book I've narrowed them down to ... ahem ... 10. It's the best I could do, and you'll see why.

I keep a range of whole-grain gluten-free flours and starches on hand and, depending on the specifics of the recipe, I use a few of them in combination. By combining at least three different gluten-free flours, you will have a product with good texture and taste. I usually go for one bulk flour (usually fine brown rice flour), a little whole-grain flour for goodness (such as buckwheat or quinoa), and a little starch (cornstarch/potato/tapioca) to bind and help keep things light. And I often add ground almonds or dried coconut to keep the moisture in and add texture.

fine brown rice flour

I use fine brown rice flour as my main bulk flour. It is made of finely ground brown rice, as the name suggests, and has a lovely mellow sweet flavor that works well in both sweet and savory baking. When you rub a little between your fingers, it should feel as smooth as wheat flour with no trace of grittiness. The more coarsely ground variety, while cheaper, leaves a gritty taste in your mouth and isn't suitable for sweet baking. Brown rice flour is less refined than white rice flour and contains more nutrients and vitamins. For years I have been saying that brown and white rice flours are interchangeable, but now I don't believe they are. Brown rice flour is more absorbent than white, so if you're using white, you will need to add a little extra. You can buy fine brown rice flour from health food stores and at selected supermarkets. Buy in small amounts and store in an airtight jar or container in your pantry or in the fridge during hot weather.

white rice flour

White rice flour is a superfine flour made from finely ground white rice and can be bought very cheaply at your local Asian grocers (in 1 pound bags) and health food stores. I don't use white rice flour very often, except when cooking bánh xèo and mung bean pancakes, but I do use it often for dusting my countertop for rolling out piecrust. Make sure you buy "rice flour" rather than "glutinous rice flour" (sometimes known as "sweet rice flour"), which is made from finely ground sticky white rice and not suitable for use in my recipes.

buckwheat flour

Buckwheat flour is made from the gluten-free grain buckwheat. Although its name suggests it's part of the wheat family, it is actually a seed from a plant in the same family as rhubarb and sorrel. It has a nutty flavor and is extremely good for you, being high in protein, iron, zinc, B vitamins, and selenium. By itself it has a tendency to become gluey in some recipes, but when paired with a lighter flour, such as brown rice flour, and a starch, like tapioca or cornstarch, its somewhat strong flavor is mellowed perfectly. Buy in small amounts from health food stores and selected supermarkets and store in an airtight jar or container in the fridge. You can also find buckwheat flour at Indian stores labeled as kuttu ka atta or okhla flour—but be sure the shop has a high turnover as buckwheat flour can go rancid quite quickly.

quinoa flour

Quinoa flour is made from the nutrient-dense "superfood" quinoa (pronounced keen-wa). It has a strong grassy flavor and is great in both sweet and savory cooking. Because it is one of the more expensive and sometimes harder to find gluten-free flours, I have limited its use in this book to just a few recipes, but I do use it a lot in my day-to-day cooking. A little goes a long way and even just a touch added with cheaper flours can help to improve the texture of baked goods. You can find quinoa flour at health food stores, but its price varies hugely, so shop around. Or, if you have access to a Vitamix or flour mill, you can grind whole quinoa grains into a fine flour yourself. Buy in small amounts and store in an airtight jar or container in the fridge to prevent it turning rancid. I also use quinoa flakes as a 100% gluten-free alternative to oats in recipes such as Anzac cookies. You can track these down at your local health food store or at selected supermarkets.

millet flour

Millet flour is just millet seeds that have been very finely ground to a fine powder. It's a high-protein flour and has a sweet but slightly bitter flavor. I tend to use millet flour more in my savory cooking, but there are a few sweet baked recipes where its flavor is complementary. You can buy millet flour for a reasonable price at health food stores and at Indian stores as bajri or bajra flour—but be sure the shop has a high turnover as millet flour can go rancid quite quickly. Buy in small amounts and store in an airtight jar or container in the fridge.

potato starch (potato flour)

The potato starch used in my recipes is made from just the starch of the potato, very finely ground, and looks a little like cornstarch. It gives a lovely lightness to baked goods and also holds lots of moisture, which is always a good thing with any gluten-free baking. You can buy it at health food stores, some supermarkets, and at most Asian grocers. Store in an airtight jar or container in your pantry.

cornstarch

Cornstarch is the finely ground endosperm of the corn kernel and not to be confused with corn (maize) flour which is used in Mexican cooking. Because of the risk of GMO with all corn products, I like to buy organic cornstarch from the health food store and always do a quick check to make sure it's gluten-free too. A lot of regular cornstarch from the supermarket contains wheat. I use cornstarch in all sorts of recipes: it's a great binder, gives a lovely lightness to baked goods, and is also great to thicken sauces and puddings, such as my almond milk pudding (see page 202). In some recipes it's totally fine to use tapioca flour instead of cornstarch (for those of you who don't eat corn), and I sometimes suggest either one. However, there are times when the results just aren't the same (almond milk pudding is a good example). Store airtight in your pantry.

tapioca flour

Called flour but really more of a starch, tapioca flour is made from the root of the cassava plant. I use it as the starch component in some of my baking, however it can turn a little gummy in recipes with a lot of moisture. You can buy tapioca flour at health food stores and Asian grocers, most commonly in 1 pound bags. Store airtight in your pantry. Most commercially made arrowroot is actually just tapioca flour, so use that if tapioca flour is hard to come by.

ground almonds

Also known as almond meal or almond flour, ground almonds are finely ground blanched almonds and are one of my favorite "flours." They add a lovely tender crumb and moisture to baked goods. Even just ¼ cup can take a gluten-free muffin from something good to something truly lovely. Ground almonds are also very high in protein, and I add them to breakfast foods such as pancakes and muffins to keep us all full until lunch. Shop around, as there can be a huge difference in prices. I buy mine from the bulk bins of my local health food store at less than half the price of the supermarket. Buy in small amounts and store in an airtight jar or container in the fridge. Or double bag and freeze if you have bought in bulk.

chickpea flour

Also known as chana or besan flour, this is made from finely ground chickpeas (garbanzo beans). It has a somewhat strong flavor so is best for savory dishes. It's used extensively in Indian cooking for pakoras and bhaji. Because of its high protein content, it holds together amazingly well and is perfect for sweetcorn + basil fritters (page 62), flatbreads (page 242), and savory piecrust (page 224). It is also well priced and easily found at your local Indian grocer or health food store. Store in an airtight

jar or container in your pantry, or in your fridge in hot weather.

other gluten-free flours

Above are the most common gluten-free flours that I use in this book. I do also use a few harder-to-find flours in my day-to-day cooking, and I think they're interesting to mention.

Teff flour, made from the highly nutritious teff grain from Eastern Africa, is thankfully becoming more and more widely available although it is incredibly pricey. It gives a lovely soft crumb and color to baked goods.

Amaranth flour, made from the tiny amaranth seed, has a strong flavor similar to that of quinoa.

Sorghum flour, made from finely ground sorghum grain, is also known as Jowar in Indian grocers where it can sometimes be found.

Coconut flour, a by-product of coconut oil, was once a very hard flour to track down but is now easily picked up at your local health food store.

Mesquite flour, or powder as it's more commonly known, is a wonderful ingredient and is made from the finely ground pods of the mesquite tree (not unlike carob). It has a sweet, chocolaty aroma, and I love using even the tiniest amount in cakes and cookies. It is very pricey, but a lovely thing to have around. It can also be added to smoothies, used to flavor maple syrup, and added to recipes such as chocolate date bliss balls (page 102) to add extra nutrients and vitamins.

sweeteners
unrefined raw sugar

The sugar I use every day is unrefined cane sugar. It's available in both at health food stores and se-lected supermarkets. It is actually semi-refined, as the cane juice is cleaned before crystallizing, but a much better alternative to highly refined white sugar. It's a step in the right direction if you are wanting a more whole-food diet but are not yet ready to use completely unrefined sugars such as rapadura and panela (which I haven't used in this book because of their low availability and high cost). Because the grain size of the unrefined cane sugar is smaller than regular raw sugar, it's great to use for a lot of the baking I do. However, I find the grain a little too large to fully dissolve when creaming butter and sugar or adding sugar to beaten egg whites, so in this instance I always blend my sugar to create a much finer grain. To do this, simply place a couple of cups of sugar in a blender and blend on high for 30–45 seconds or until it's white and almost as powdery as powdered sugar. Use immediately or store in an airtight jar or container. It does have a tendency to clump if stored for long periods once blended, so might need sifting or another quick blend before using. This is what I mean in recipes that list "blended unrefined raw sugar." This can also be used in place of powdered sugar for dusting cakes.

muscovado sugar

Muscovado sugar is a semi-unrefined cane sugar that still contains the molasses in varying degrees and has more nutrients than regular soft brown sugar (which is really just refined white sugar with some of the molasses added to turn it brown). If you can't track down muscovado sugar, soft brown sugar is your next best choice. Muscovado comes in either light or dark and I tend to use light. It has a tendency to clump together so break it up with your fingers. Store airtight in your pantry and do note that if left opened for long periods it can dry out, making it not great for baking, but still fine for spiced hot chocolate (page 170). Buy it at health food stores and selected supermarkets.

brown rice syrup

Sometimes referred to on the label as brown rice malt syrup, this is a sweet (but not in-your-face-so) sticky syrup made from cooked brown rice flour or brown rice starch and enzymes. It's considered one of the most "whole" natural sweeteners out there and is one of my favorites to use. It has the same consistency as honey but is less sweet. It can be found at health food stores and at selected supermarkets for a very reasonable price. If you have celiac disease or are ultrasensitive to gluten, make sure you source certified gluten-free brown rice syrup (or use honey), as some brands are made in factories where wheat is handled. Store airtight in the pantry.

maple syrup

I always buy 100% pure maple syrup; imitation maple syrup is mostly just cane sugar with flavors and colors added in. It's not the cheapest pantry good, but its flavor is beautiful. Store in the fridge once opened.

honey

I buy a local honey that has a beautiful floral sweet flavor. Store airtight in your pantry.

dates

I often use dates to naturally sweeten baked goods and raw treats. I love eating Medjool dates for a natural caramel hit. However, they can be pricey, so I've only used the more readily available pitted dried dates in this book.

fats

butter

I grew up in a household where using margarine was pretty much as bad as saying a swear word. It was such a great relief when I successfully reintroduced real butter into our diets a few years ago: nothing beats butter in flavor, and it's what I use most often for baking. Use salted or unsalted butter for the recipes in this book.

ghee (clarified butter)

Ghee heats to a high temperature without burning and gives a lovely buttery flavor to foods, without the lactose. I use it to panfry, sauté, and sometimes even in baking. Because it has no milk solids, it keeps well for up to 2 months in a jar at room temperature (although I make fairly small 1-pound batches that last about 3–4 weeks). Most people tend to use unsalted butter when making ghee, but I generally use regular salted butter. Most of the salt stays in the sediment at the bottom of the pan and is discarded anyway.

To make ghee, put 1 pound salted or unsalted butter in a saucepan—when it melts, it will foam up, so allow room for this in your pan. Gently melt over low-medium heat, stirring occasionally until starting to boil. Reduce heat to low and simmer gently for around 10 minutes. If you have a splatter screen, now is a good time to use it as the butter will spit a little. After about 10 minutes the splattering will have subsided, the

invaluable as the setting agent in all raw sweet treats, as it firms up to solid when chilled. Virgin coconut oil also has a magical ability to soften the somewhat grassy flavor of avocado in my chocolate avocado tart (page 192) and lessens the "green" flavor of the Swiss chard in the green smoothie (page 50). In winter it will set solid, so heat gently until liquid once again before adding to a recipe.

olive oil

I use olive oil for cooking and reserve my more expensive extra-virgin olive oils for finishing off a dish, to drizzle, or to use in salad dressings.

pure sesame oil

I keep a little bottle of pure sesame oil in my fridge for use in Asian dishes, where a little goes a very long way.

rice bran + grapeseed oils

I used to use rice bran and grapeseed oils when I wanted flavorless oil. However, recently it's become much clearer how these oils are extracted using solvents, so I no longer buy or use either of them.

milk solids dropped to the bottom of the pan and turned light golden brown, and there will still be just a little foam on the surface. Remove from the heat and set aside for 10 minutes before straining through a fine sieve into a glass jar, leaving behind the sediment in the bottom of the pan. Allow to cool before putting on the lid. Store either at room temperature or in the fridge. Makes approx. 1½ cups (375 ml).

virgin coconut oil

Virgin coconut oil is another of my favorite fats to use. It's extremely good for you and a very stable nondairy fat to use in high-heat cooking. I use it in Asian and Indian cooking, and it's

rice, rice, and more rice . . . and some grains, seeds, nuts + legumes, too

rice

We live off rice and not just because of my husband's Vietnamese background. It's cheap, easy to prepare, and can be eaten at any time of the day. Our main types are: white jasmine, medium brown, white basmati, and black rice for puddings. I grew up on brown rice and was a teenager before I ate white rice. I adore brown rice for its higher nutrient content, nutty flavor, and because it reminds me of home, but when it comes to Asian or Indian food, I do prefer the flavor and texture of white jasmine or basmati rice. I believe in the teachings of Chinese and Ayurvedic medicine, which promote eating white rice over brown as it's much gentler on our digestive system. You eat whichever you prefer; I personally like to just mix things up and eat a bit of each.

white rice

Eating an Indian curry would not be the same without a pile of freshly cooked white basmati rice on the side. However, because we eat Asian-style, it's white jasmine rice that we go through the most.

To cook white rice, put 1 cup (215 g) white rice (jasmine or basmati) in a saucepan, cover with plenty of water, and scrunch and massage the grains with your hands to release the excess starch. Drain the cloudy water off and repeat a couple more times until the water is relatively clear. Drain rice well and put back in the pan. Add 1¼ cups (310 ml) cold water to the pan, cover with a tight-fitting lid (it's very helpful if it's glass) and place over high heat. The second the water comes to a boil, reduce the heat to the lowest setting without disturbing the rice or lid at all and cook for 12–14 minutes until all the water has been absorbed and there are little tunnels formed in the rice. Remove from the heat, keeping the lid firmly on, and set aside for 10 minutes before fluffing up the rice with a fork to serve. This is the amount that I cook for two adults and two kids (about 3 cups cooked rice); however, if you're feeding a crowd, you can double or triple this amount. If you do so, you can scale back the ratio of water to rice—use the same amount as the rice with just an extra few tablespoons of water. So for 2 cups rice I would use 2¼ cups water (not 2½ cups).

brown rice

To cook brown rice, wash and drain 1 cup (200 g) brown rice (medium grain, jasmine, or basmati) and place in a pan with 1¾ cups (435 ml) cold water, cover with a tight-fitting lid and bring to a boil. Reduce heat to the lowest setting and simmer, covered, for about 40–45 minutes until the water is absorbed and the rice tender. Remove from the heat, keeping the lid on, and allow it to stand for 10 minutes before serving. This is the amount that I cook for two adults and two kids (about 3 cups cooked rice).

buckwheat

Although the name suggests it is part of the wheat family, buckwheat is actually a grain from the same family as rhubarb and sorrel. It has a nutty flavor and is extremely good for you, being high in protein, iron, zinc, B vitamins, and selenium. It's great in salads or stews and forms the key ingredient in my tabouli recipe (page 82).

To cook buckwheat, bring 2 cups (500 ml) cold water and a pinch of sea salt to a boil in a saucepan. Add 1 cup (180 g) raw hulled buckwheat, reduce heat to a simmer, cover and cook for 15–20 minutes or until the water is absorbed and the buckwheat tender. Remove the lid in

the last few minutes of cooking to allow excess liquid to evaporate if needed. Remove from the heat, cover with the lid slightly ajar, and allow to cool. Fluff up with a fork. This is about the right amount for 4 people (3 cups of cooked buckwheat).

quinoa

Quinoa is labeled as a superfood and for good reason. It's ridiculously high in protein, and unlike most other vegetarian protein sources, it actually contains all of the 9 essential amino acids, meaning it's a complete protein. It's high in iron, calcium, B vitamins, and fiber, and while it's not the cheapest food, a little does go a long way. You can buy quinoa in shades of black, red, and brown; they all work and cook the same, although I find the black and red varieties have a slightly stronger nutty flavor. I often make porridge out of it and love adding it to salads (page 86, quinoa asparagus salad) or serving it with stews. I find the easiest way to rinse the teeny little quinoa grains is to place them in a fine sieve and run cold water over them while stirring them around a bit. Most quinoa is pre-rinsed these days, but most varieties will require at least 3–4 good rinses to remove the naturally bitter saponin coating.

To cook quinoa, bring 1½ cups (375 ml) water to a boil in a saucepan, add 1 cup (185 g) quinoa, cover with a lid, and reduce the heat to a gentle simmer. Cook for 10–12 minutes until all the water has been absorbed and the quinoa is tender. Remove from the heat, leave the lid on, and set aside to steam for another 5 minutes before fluffing up with a fork. This makes about enough for 4 people (3 cups cooked quinoa).

millet

Millet is one of those underrated grains that I adore but, to be quite blunt, it's mostly known for its addition to birdseed. The upside to this is that it's one of the cheapest gluten-free grains on the market, and I'd be really happy if it stayed that way. Throughout winter I have a container of cooked millet in the fridge that I use to make warm millet with berry-bay compote (page 42) in the morning, and I love adding it to salads or with roasted vegetables for a hit of goodness. Like buckwheat and quinoa, millet is high in protein, calcium, iron, B vitamins, and zinc, but it has a weaker flavor and is a great substitute for rice if you're looking to eat more nutrient-dense foods. You can just simmer the grains in water; however, I really like the flavor and texture if lightly toasted in a little oil or ghee first.

To make about 3 cups cooked millet, heat 1 tablespoon virgin coconut oil, olive oil, or ghee in a saucepan, add 1 cup (210 g) raw hulled millet and stir constantly for 3–4 minutes until it smells toasty. Carefully add 2 cups (500 ml) water (it will splutter a bit) and a pinch of salt, cover the pan, and bring to a boil. Reduce the heat to the lowest setting and simmer for 20 minutes, by which time all the water will have been absorbed and the millet will be tender. Remove from the heat, keep the lid on, and allow to sit for 5 minutes before fluffing up with a fork.

toasting spices, seeds + nuts

Toast whole spices in a dry pan over medium heat, stirring often, for 30–60 seconds or until lightly browned. Remove from the heat and grind to a fine powder using a mortar and pestle or spice grinder.

Toast sesame seeds or pine nuts in a dry frying pan over medium heat for 1–2 minutes, stirring constantly until light golden all over. Watch them like a hawk, as they go from golden to black in a matter of seconds.

To lightly toast cashews or whole almonds, bake at 350°F (180°C) for 10–12 minutes, stirring every 5 minutes until golden brown. Toast sliced almonds for just 4–5 minutes; and pecans for 8–10 minutes.

To lightly toast whole peanuts, bake at 350°F (180°C) for 12–15 minutes, stirring every 5 minutes until golden brown and skins start to lift off. You can rub the skins off when cool, if preferred.

legumes

Sitting alongside the jars of grains and seeds in my pantry, you'll find legumes of every color and shape. I have a tendency to buy every legume I ever come across, but the main ones I use are chickpeas, lentils, and butterbeans.

I buy regular brown lentils, which are always cheap, but also have a thing for French Puy-style lentils as they keep their shape and texture once cooked. I keep a well-stocked jar of red lentils and use these often for soups and dhals, and I buy whole dried chickpeas to use in stews, soups, or to make into falafel and hummus.

I always have dried mung beans, both whole and split (moong dhal); the whole ones I sprout and add to salads or soak and use to make pancakes (page 68), while the split ones go into dhal or are soaked overnight and added raw to salads. Make sure you buy un-heat-treated legumes or you'll never get them soft no matter how long you soak and cook them. And, although they are not my first choice, I also keep a few tins of cooked chickpeas and butterbeans for times when I haven't planned ahead. Just make sure you rinse and drain them well before use.

dairy alternatives + eggs

We eat very little dairy in our family as lactose is not really our friend. Listed below are the low-lactose dairy products we can tolerate and also the dairy-free alternatives that I like to use at home. I've lumped eggs into this category too, but please don't assume that if you can't tolerate one, you can't tolerate the other. We eat very little dairy in our house, but we go through a carton of eggs in the blink of an eye!

yogurt

I make my own natural yogurt for a fraction of the cost of store-bought (page 220). If you are buying yours, go for a natural plain yogurt or thick unsweetened Greek yogurt. Most of the lactose is broken down into lactic acid, so some people, like us, can enjoy it with no problems.

labneh

Labneh is strained yogurt and a great alternative to cream cheese or cream when lactose is not tolerated. You can find it at selected specialty stores, but it's really easy to make yourself (page 222) and very cost-effective to make if using homemade yogurt.

feta

Feta is one of the only cheeses we tolerate, with the odd exception of a little bit of mozzarella. I buy both firm Greek-style feta and soft Danish feta.

coconut milk + cream

We go through lots of coconut milk and cream in our house. I do sometimes make my own by blending peeled mature coconut flesh with warm water and straining it through my nut-milk bag (cheesecloth or muslin can also be used). Usually, I just buy the canned stuff. When buying canned coconut milk and cream it is important that you read the label. It should list only coconut and water (and sometimes ascorbic acid, which is just vitamin C used as a natural preservative). Many brands, even some organic ones, contain emulsifiers, thickeners, and preservatives. I recommend you always buy full-fat too: the light varieties are simply thinned down with water and then thickeners and emulsifiers are put back in to give the same mouthfeel as full-fat. If you like, you can always use a mixture of half coconut milk/cream, half water, making the overall fat content less (but also lessening the deliciousness, in my humble opinion).

whipped coconut cream

This is a great alternative to whipped cream for the lactose intolerant. You might have to experiment with different brands of coconut milk to find out which ones set firm in the fridge, as not all do. I find AROY-D brand works well—it is made in Thailand and found at your local Asian grocers.

Refrigerate the can overnight and then give it a gentle shake. If you don't hear any movement in the can, you should be good to go. If there is movement, reserve that can for another use and try a different brand. Open the can, scrape off the solid top layer of "cream," and place into a clean bowl. Reserve the watery liquid from the bottom for another use (add to your morning porridge in place of milk or use in smoothies). Whisk the cream for 1–2 minutes with electric beaters or a balloon whisk, until thick like regular whipped cream. Sweeten to taste with a touch of honey, maple syrup, or powdered sugar, keeping in mind that you're usually serving with a sweet dessert.

nut + rice milk

The main milks I use are homemade almond milk and store-bought rice milk. You can buy almond milk, but many contain questionable ingredients such as carrageenan and high-fructose sweeteners such as agave syrup. It's so easy to make it yourself that I can't recommend it enough. Most commercially made almond milks also contain high amounts of phytic acid as the nuts are not always soaked before the milk is made. I have to admit I don't always soak *all* the nuts that I eat; however, if you are consuming large amounts of commercially made almond milk, you'd be getting a pretty large daily dose of these enzyme inhibitors. I make almond milk every few days and store it in the fridge in a large glass jar (just shake before using as the solids will settle to the bottom), and I always have cartons of unsweetened local-made rice milk (both regular and the high-protein version where chickpeas are added) on hand for use in baking and for times when I haven't made fresh almond milk.

You will find a recipe for almond milk on page 162, and walnut and maple milk on page 164.

Another favorite is cashew milk made with a little hint of vanilla bean paste or extract (great for use in chia pudding, see page 54), or for a cheaper version use a mixture of almonds and sunflower or pumpkin (pepita) seeds. To make chocolate or carob milk (my kids' favorite) simply blend your favorite nut milk with a little cocoa or carob powder and a touch of pure maple or brown rice syrup to taste.

To make other nut milks, use the same ratio of 1 cup nuts to 3 cups water for a thick creamy milk, or add 1 more cup of water to make a thinner budget-friendly version. Cashews will make about the same amount of milk as walnuts. However, when making almond milk (using 3 cups of water), you will get slightly less milk and more leftover pulp, due to the fibrous skins.

free-range eggs

We eat eggs so quickly in our house that I just leave them out on the counter, with the exception of high summer when I keep them in the fridge. I recommend you bring your eggs to room temperature for baking; this helps the eggs emulsify with the other ingredients and gives better rise. Either leave out on the counter overnight, or set them in a bowl of warm water for 5 minutes before using. Because I buy my eggs straight from the farmer, they tend to be large or extra-large size.

other bits + bobs . . .
cocoa powder

I use regular natural unsweetened (non-alkalized) cocoa powder, not Dutch-processed cocoa.

psyllium husks

More commonly used as a dietary fiber supplement, psyllium husks are amazing in gluten-free baked goods, especially breads. I use them in conjunction with ground flaxseeds and chia seeds in place of xanthan and guar gums in my gluten-free breads. They suck up moisture and give breads good elasticity to prevent cracking and crumbling. Buy from the health food section of most supermarkets or your local health food store. As you only use in small amounts, one 1 pound bag will last you a very long time. Store airtight once opened.

tahini

Tahini is a wonderful dairy-free source of calcium. If you can handle the more intense flavor of the unhulled, you'll be gaining higher nutritional values. Store tahini in the fridge once opened to prevent the oils from turning rancid.

kefir

If you suffer from celiac disease or food intolerances, the single most important thing I'd recommend including in your diet to help heal your delicate digestive system is kefir (pronounced ka-fear). Kefir is available in both milk and water form and, while I have had both grains in the past, it is the water kefir that I prefer (there is a recipe for ginger kefir water on page 172). As a family who doesn't often keep cow's milk in the fridge, trying to remember to buy it to make milk kefir was a little too hard. For water kefir all that's needed is water, sugar, and dried fruit—too easy.

Kefir water contains loads of beneficial probiotics that help create a healthier digestive system. It's also packed to the brim with good bacteria, beneficial yeasts, vitamins, minerals, amino acids, and enzymes. Because it's not commercially available, you do have to hunt around a little to find the grains, but if looked after correctly, you will have a lifetime supply of kefir and as the grains multiply you'll have plenty to pass on to family and friends. If you're new to kefir, a quick Internet search might pull up someone selling or giving away their excess kefir grains in your area.

Just as with pets, there's always a worry about what to do with your kefir grains when you're on holiday. If you don't have a friend willing to look after them, I've got you sorted. Just before you go, strain and feed your kefir as per normal but with at least double the usual amount of sugar and dried fruit. Put the lid on and place in the fridge. When you arrive home from your holiday (the longest I've left mine is 3 weeks), strain off the liquid and discard. Feed as normal and continue with this cycle of brewing, discarding, and feeding the water kefir every few days for at least 1 week or until it looks healthy again with lots of visible bubble activity before drinking.

RISE + SHINE

Breakfast has always been my favorite meal of the day. Now that both my kids are school age, our weekday morning ritual is a somewhat chaotic mishmash of finding school uniforms, gobbling down breakfast, brushing teeth and hair, and tying shoelaces. But I still love the food of breakfast, even when it has to be eaten fast.

In summer we eat loads of fruit salads and green smoothies, but come winter a bowl of steaming millet porridge is all I crave. I know I'm not the only one who is racing around in the morning in these busy times, so I've tried to keep these recipes simple and let you know which parts can be made in advance, freeing you up to enjoy more of the madness that is the weekday morning. On Sundays, pancakes and crepes are firmly back on the menu, and we all kick about in our pajamas for as long as possible.

I start the day with a glass of lemon water, just like my mama always preached. It seems to get my whole system started, and it's a great way to use up all those naked lemons that are hanging around in my fridge after I've stolen their zest.

BUCKWHEAT BANANA + BERRY PANCAKES
MAKES 12–14 SMALL PANCAKES OR 8 LARGE ONES

These barely sweet pancakes are our go-to Sunday morning breakfast, but if the kids had their way, we'd be eating them every morning. I add banana and berries to the pancakes when they're cooking—I love how the banana softens and caramelizes and the berries intensify in flavor. I don't usually add any sweetener as I find the banana and maple syrup more than enough first thing in the morning, but you could add 1–2 teaspoons unrefined raw sugar or honey to the batter when mixing.

¾ cup (105 g) buckwheat flour

¾ cup (105 g) fine brown rice flour

4 teaspoons gluten-free baking powder

¾ cup (80 g) ground almonds

3 large free-range eggs

1 tablespoon melted ghee, olive or coconut oil + extra, to cook

1 teaspoon vanilla extract

1½ cups (375 ml) almond, rice or coconut milk + extra, as needed

2 bananas, sliced

1 cup (125 g) mixed berries, fresh or frozen

Maple syrup or honey, thick Greek yogurt + lemon wedges, to serve

+ Sift buckwheat flour, brown rice flour, and baking powder into a bowl and whisk in ground almonds and a pinch of fine sea salt. (Add sugar now, if you are using.) In another smaller bowl, whisk together eggs, ghee, vanilla, and milk. Pour into the dry ingredients and whisk to a smooth-ish batter. If you have time (but, to be honest, I very rarely do), cover and set aside at room temperature for 15–20 minutes before cooking.

+ Heat a little ghee or oil in a heavy-bottomed frying pan over medium heat. Drop ¼–⅓ cup batter into the pan (depending on whether you want child- or adult-sized pancakes). I don't bother spreading the batter as I like my pancakes thick and fluffy.

+ Top each pancake with a few slices of banana and 3–4 berries and cook until bubbles appear on the surface and the bottom is golden. Flip with a wide metal spatula and cook for another 1–2 minutes until golden and cooked through. Serve pancakes with maple syrup or honey, thick Greek yogurt, and lemon wedges.

TOFU SCRAMBLE WITH CHIPOTLE SAUCE SERVES 4

Tofu scramble came into vogue when I was a teenager, coinciding with the new vegan lifestyle adopted by many of the girls I hung out with. Back then I never had the dedication to pull off such a lifestyle (the thought of going without chocolate was enough to make me stick to my vegetarian diet without question). All that said, you certainly don't need to be vegan to enjoy tofu scramble. Tofu contains loads of protein, which, when paired with sourdough bread, helps keep you feeling full all morning. The recipe for chipotle sauce will make nearly double what you need here, but it keeps in the fridge for at least a week. You can find little cans of chipotle chilies in adobo sauce at some supermarkets or specialty food stores, or, if all else fails, simply serve this scramble with your favorite hot sauce.

3 tablespoons olive oil or ghee

2 garlic cloves, crushed

1 teaspoon ground cumin

24 ounces (700 g) firm tofu, drained, patted dry + roughly crumbled into bite-sized chunks

Hot buttered sourdough toast, to serve

Juice of ½ lime + lime wedges, to serve

1 spring onion, finely sliced, to serve

Small handful of cilantro, to serve

chipotle sauce

Half 7-ounce (100 g) can chipotle chilies in adobo sauce or hot sauce to taste

2 small garlic cloves

½ cup (125 ml) water

+ To make the chipotle sauce, blend chilies, garlic, and ½ cup (125 ml) water in a blender or food processor until smooth. Season to taste with sea salt.

+ Heat a large heavy-bottomed frying pan over medium heat. Add oil or ghee and sauté garlic and cumin for 30 seconds, stirring until fragrant. Add crumbled tofu and stir-fry for 4–5 minutes, using a metal spatula to scrape any crispy bits from the bottom of the pan. Once lightly golden and warmed through, remove tofu from heat, season to taste with sea salt and plenty of freshly ground black pepper. Spoon over toast, drizzle with a little chipotle sauce and lime juice, scatter over spring onion and cilantro, and serve with lime wedges.

QUINOA CREPES WITH ORANGE MAPLE SAUCE MAKES 8–10 CREPES

As much as I love pancakes (and I really do love them), I adore the thinness and lightness of crepes. This batter keeps well overnight, covered in the fridge, making breakfast much speedier. Just give it a good stir before cooking. The sauce can also be made in advance and stored in a glass jar for 2–3 days. The ghee/oil will rise and set on the top, so just reheat it briefly until melted before serving. To serve these crepes with a savory filling, omit the vanilla and add a little extra salt and pepper to the mix.

The quinoa flour makes for a beautiful tender crepe. Buckwheat flour works too, if that's what you have in your cupboard—just let the batter rest for at least an hour and don't be alarmed by the somewhat gluey texture and gray color of buckwheat batter.

1 cup (120 g) quinoa flour

3 large free-range eggs

1 teaspoon vanilla extract

2 tablespoons olive or coconut oil or melted ghee + extra, to cook

1¼ cups (310 ml) rice or almond milk

Natural plain yogurt, to serve

orange maple sauce

½ cup (125 ml) pure maple syrup

2 tablespoons virgin coconut oil or ghee

Finely grated zest and juice of 1 orange

1 orange, segmented (see NOTE)

+ Sift flour and a good pinch of fine sea salt into a bowl. In a smaller bowl, whisk together eggs, vanilla, oil, and milk. Add to flour and whisk to a smooth batter. Pour through a fine sieve set over a measuring cup or bowl and use the back of a metal spoon to press out any small lumps. Cover and set aside at room temperature for at least 30 minutes, or in the fridge overnight.

+ To make orange maple sauce, heat maple syrup and oil in a small saucepan over medium heat until oil has melted. Increase heat and boil for 1 minute. Add orange zest and juice, bring back to a boil then reduce to a simmer and cook for 6–8 minutes or until syrupy. Strain over the orange segments through a fine sieve, squeezing as much flavor and goodness as you can from the zest before discarding it.

+ Heat an 8-inch frying pan over medium-high heat. Add the teeniest bit of oil or ghee, swirling the pan to coat evenly (tip out any excess if you need to). Pour in ¼ cup of batter, tilting the pan to evenly coat with a very thin layer of batter. Cook for 30–45 seconds or until the underside is golden and the edge starts to lift away from the side of the pan. Flip with a metal spatula or palette knife and cook through for another 15–30 seconds. Transfer to a plate. Cook the remaining batter, stacking crepes on top of each other and covering with a clean tea towel. Serve with orange maple sauce and natural plain yogurt.

NOTE: To neatly segment an orange, you will need a small sharp knife, a cutting board and a bowl. Slice a small round off the top and bottom of the orange to create a flat surface and stand the orange upright on your board. Use your knife to cut off thick slices of peel (and as much of the bitter white pith as you can) in a downward motion following the contours of the orange. Once the orange is free from all peel and pith, place in the palm of your nondominant hand. Make a cut straight down the side of one of the segments, cutting right between the membrane and the flesh at a slight angle. Do the same on the other side of the segment to release it, and drop it into the bowl. Remove all the segments until you are left with the naked membrane in your hand. Squeeze any juice left in the membrane over the slices in the bowl.

MILLET + FLAXSEED PORRIDGE WITH ORANGE PRUNES SERVES 4

When I was growing up, Mum used to make two types of porridge: the standard, stick-to-your-ribs oat porridge that plopped away happily on the stove forever; and this one, which we called birdseed porridge. She would make enough for herself, Dad, and my older sister Jessie—the only ones who liked it back then.

You can buy millet meal at health food stores and some supermarkets but, just like my mum used to do, I grind my own raw hulled millet and flaxseed in a blender until it forms a rough meal. (A small coffee grinder would also work.) I make enough to last me the week and then store it in a glass jar in the fridge. Millet and flaxseed meal can easily turn rancid so grinding your own guarantees freshness.

I've made a few changes to my mum's original recipe, adding banana and a little bit of coconut oil to the pot to naturally sweeten and give a lovely texture to the otherwise silky smooth porridge. The coconut oil also helps to mask the slightly bitter flavor of the millet meal.

You will need to start the night before if you're planning on serving this with the orange prunes, although I love it just as much served plain.

1 cup (145 g) millet meal
2 tablespoons (12 g) ground flaxseeds (see NOTE)
2 cups (500 ml) almond or rice milk
2 tablespoons virgin coconut oil, melted (optional)
2 bananas, peeled and thinly sliced (optional)
2 cups (500 ml) cold water
Honey or brown rice syrup, to taste (optional)

orange prunes
1 cup (200 g) natural pitted prunes, roughly chopped
¾ cup (185 ml) freshly squeezed orange juice

+ To make orange prunes, combine prunes and orange juice in a glass jar or container. Stir well, cover, and pop in the fridge overnight. If you're in a hurry in the morning and have forgotten to soak the prunes overnight, you can gently heat the prunes and juice in a saucepan over low heat until most of the juice is absorbed and syrupy (but I prefer the texture of the overnight ones).

+ To make porridge, place millet meal, flaxseed, milk, coconut oil, and sliced bananas into a saucepan with 2 cups (500 ml) cold water and a pinch of fine sea salt. Bring to a boil, stirring constantly to prevent lumps forming. Reduce to a simmer and cook, stirring often, for 8–10 minutes until thick and creamy (this may only take around 5 minutes if you are using a really finely ground store-bought millet meal). Add a little more liquid if needed. Have a taste and sweeten with a spoonful of honey or brown rice syrup if you like, keeping in mind that the prunes will add natural sweetness of their own.

+ Serve hot, topped with a few spoonfuls of orange prunes and their syrup.

NOTE: I use regular brown flaxseeds for this porridge, as I find golden flaxseeds tend to get a little gluey. If you only have golden, use just 1 tablespoon rather than two.

TAHINI, ORANGE + COCONUT TOASTED MUESLI MAKES 2 POUNDS

Muesli-making was always my dad's domain when we were little. Late at night he would set himself up in the kitchen, toasting and chopping like a mad man, before decanting the goods into his giant glass muesli jar. I remember him saying how expensive it was to make but, and this is a huge BUT, homemade muesli beats that store-bought sweetened stuff hands down. This is my favorite version, and it's filled to the brim with the goodness of quinoa flakes, shredded coconut, nuts, and fruit all bound together in a sweet (but not in-your-face-sweet) mixture of coconut oil, tahini, honey, and orange zest. To keep things strictly vegan you can use pure maple or brown rice syrup in place of the honey. Also, whole-grain oats can be used in place of the quinoa flakes.

5 cups (500 g) quinoa flakes

2 cups (180 g) shredded or flaked coconut

½ cup (65 g) cashews, roughly chopped

½ cup (75 g) whole raw almonds, roughly chopped

½ cup (65 g) pumpkin seeds (pepitas)

½ cup (60 g) sunflower seeds

¼ cup (35 g) sesame seeds

⅓ cup (80 ml) virgin coconut oil

⅓ cup (80 ml) honey, pure maple or brown rice syrup

⅓ cup (80 ml) unhulled tahini

1 teaspoon vanilla extract

Finely grated zest of 2 oranges

½ teaspoon fine sea salt

1 cup (200 g) natural raisins or sultanas

1½ cups (165 g) dried cranberries

1 cup (95 g) firmly packed dried apple slices, roughly chopped

½ cup (80 g) pitted dried dates, roughly chopped

+ Preheat oven to 350°F (180°C). Combine quinoa flakes, coconut, cashews, almonds, pumpkin seeds, sunflower, and sesame seeds in a large bowl, using your hands to mix thoroughly. Combine coconut oil, honey or syrup, tahini, vanilla, orange zest, and sea salt in a small pan and bring slowly to a boil, stirring constantly until melted and combined. Pour over dry ingredients and mix well.

+ Transfer to a large deep baking sheet and bake for 25–30 minutes, stirring every 10 minutes, until toasty and golden brown. Watch those edges like a hawk as they have a tendency to burn. Remove from the oven and set aside to cool. Stir in the dried fruit and transfer to a large glass jar or airtight container. Will keep for 2–3 weeks as long as airtight.

NUT PORRIDGE SERVES 4–5

It was always a good sign when I saw the little bowls of dried fruit and nuts sitting out to soak on the kitchen counter last thing at night. I would go to bed knowing that daybreak would bring one of my favorite breakfasts, something we kids affectionately called "fruit + nut whip." It's a very simple recipe: nuts, seeds, and dried fruit all soaked overnight and then blitzed together until smooth. You can use any combination of fruit, seeds, and nuts, but I reckon you need a few cashews in there for the creaminess they bring. Also try to source natural or organic raisins—most regular ones are coated in glycerin and hydrogenated vegetable oil to prevent them sticking during processing.

1 cup (125 g) sunflower seeds

½ cup (65 g) pumpkin seeds (pepitas)

1 cup (125 g) raw cashews

½ cup (75 g) whole raw almonds

3 pieces dried pear or ¼ cup (40 g) dried pitted dates or apricots

¼ cup (50 g) natural raisins

1 cup (250 ml) water

¼–½ cup (60–80 ml) freshly squeezed orange juice or water

Natural plain yogurt, fresh fruit, honey/pure maple syrup, flaked almonds, dried currants, and finely grated orange zest, to serve (optional)

+ Set out 3 medium-sized glass or ceramic bowls. Place the sunflower and pumpkin seeds in one bowl, cashews, and almonds in another, and dried fruit in the last one. Pour enough cold water into each bowl to fully cover the nuts/seeds/fruit. Drape a clean tea towel over the three bowls and soak at room temperature overnight (or in the fridge in hot weather).

+ Drain nuts, seeds, and fruit and transfer to a blender. Add 1 cup (250ml) water and the orange juice (or extra water) and blend on high to form a relatively smooth paste. You may need to stop a few times and stir or scrape down the side of the bowl, encouraging everything to blend evenly. Add more orange juice or water if you want a thinner consistency or if your blender is straining. Spoon into 4–5 bowls and top with yogurt, fresh fruit, honey or pure maple syrup, flaked almonds, dried currants, and orange zest. The porridge is best made and eaten fresh, but leftovers will keep in an airtight container in the fridge for 2–3 days.

BUCKWHEAT PANCAKES WITH HORSERADISH YOGURT + BEETS

MAKES 12 SMALL PANCAKES

I love buckwheat blinis, those gloriously light and fluffy yeasted pancakes that hail from Russia. But they do have a tendency to be temperamental. If you don't prove the batter for the exact amount of time or beat out too much air when folding in the egg whites, you end up with disappointing flat rounds of dough. This is what always used to happen to me, so here is my cop-out version; more like a pancake than blini with its absence of yeast, but still with all that lightness that I love. These are topped with horseradish yogurt and thin slices of beets, but they also work brilliantly under creamy scrambled eggs, or sweetened up with a smear of tahini and a drizzle of honey. Or go traditional and serve for morning tea with a dollop of jam and softly whipped cream.

½ cup (70 g) buckwheat flour

¼ cup (35 g) fine brown rice flour

¼ cup (40 g) potato flour

1½ teaspoons gluten-free baking powder

½ teaspoon fine sea salt

¾ cup (185 ml) almond or rice milk

1 teaspoon apple cider vinegar

1 large free-range egg, separated

Olive oil or ghee

horseradish yogurt

1 cup (250 g) natural plain yogurt

1 tablespoon horseradish cream (see NOTE)

Finely grated zest of ½ lemon

beets

8–10 baby beets, washed + stalks trimmed to approx. 1 inch long

1 tablespoon lemon juice

1 tablespoon extra-virgin olive oil

Small handful of dill, roughly torn, to serve

Lemon wedges, to serve

+ The pancakes themselves are quick to make, so prepare the toppings first. For the beets, place beets in a small saucepan, cover with plenty of water, and bring to a boil. Reduce to a simmer and cook for 20–30 minutes or until tender. Drain and cool slightly. When cold enough to handle, peel, thinly slice, and place in a bowl. Drizzle with lemon juice and olive oil and season well with sea salt and freshly ground black pepper.

+ To make horseradish yogurt, combine all ingredients in a small bowl and season with fine sea salt and freshly ground black pepper.

+ To make pancakes, sift flours, baking powder, and salt into a bowl. Combine milk and cider vinegar in a measuring cup and set aside for a few minutes until curdled slightly (very noticeable with rice milk, not so much with almond milk). Add egg yolk and whisk well. Pour into dry ingredients and whisk until a smooth batter forms.

+ Using an electric mixer or balloon whisk, whisk egg white in a clean dry bowl until stiff peaks form. Use a metal spoon to gently fold one-third of the egg white into the batter to loosen it before very gently folding in the remaining white just until combined (a few little lumps of egg white here and there are totally fine).

+ Heat a large frying pan over medium heat and add a little olive oil or ghee, swirling to coat. Drop large spoonfuls of batter into the pan and cook for 1–2 minutes until bubbles show on the top and the underside is golden. Flip over with a wide metal spatula and cook for another 1 minute or until cooked through. Transfer to a wire rack while you cook the remaining batter.

+ Smear a dollop of horseradish yogurt over each pancake, top with a few slices of beets and torn dill, and serve with lemon wedges.

NOTE: If you have celiac disease or are super-intolerant to gluten, try to source gluten-free horseradish cream. If you can track down fresh horseradish, use that finely grated instead.

WARM MILLET WITH BERRY-BAY COMPOTE SERVES 4

This is one of my favorite breakfasts to make on a cool winter morning. Before I hear you scoff "who has time to cook millet from scratch in the morning?", I'll let you in on a little secret: I cook up a big pot of millet at the start of the week and keep it in the fridge in a glass container. In the morning I take out a portion (or two), add a little almond milk and lemon zest, and give it a quick blast on the stovetop until creamy. If you are very organized, you can cook the berry-bay compote at the same time as the millet and place them right next to each other in the fridge for easy access!

To make this vegan, use unrefined raw sugar or brown rice syrup in place of honey in the compote. If you're using frozen berries, try to source locally grown ones (even better, organic). Or do as I do, and stock up on berries at the peak of summer when they're cheap and freeze them in bags to use throughout the year.

1 tablespoon virgin
    coconut oil
1 cup (210 g) raw hulled
    millet
2 cups (500 ml) water
Finely grated zest of
    1 lemon
1½–2 cups (375–500 ml)
    almond, rice, or coconut
    milk + extra, to serve

berry-bay compote
2 cups (250 g) mixed fresh
    or frozen berries
2 bay leaves, fresh or dried
¼ cup (60 ml) honey

+ Heat coconut oil in a saucepan, add millet, and stir for 3–4 minutes or until toasty smelling. Carefully add 2 cups (500 ml) water (it will splutter a bit) and a pinch of salt, cover pan, and bring to a boil. Reduce heat to the lowest setting and simmer for 20 minutes, by which time all the water will have been absorbed and the millet will be tender. Remove from the heat, keep the lid on, and let sit for 5 minutes before fluffing up with a fork. At this stage you can cool the millet and store it in a covered container in the fridge for 3–4 days, or continue on with the recipe.

+ Add lemon zest and 1½ cups milk to the cooked millet. Bring back to a boil, reduce the heat, and simmer for 5–10 minutes, adding more milk as needed until the millet is warmed through and slightly creamy. (If you're using cold cooked millet from the fridge, you might need to break up the lumps with a wooden spoon as it cooks.) Serve in bowls with berry-bay compote and perhaps an extra splash of milk.

+ To make the berry-bay compote, place berries, bay leaves, and honey in a saucepan and bring to a boil, stirring to dissolve the honey. Reduce the heat and simmer for 8–10 minutes until thickened slightly and syrupy. Remove from the heat. I like to leave the bay leaves in as long as possible to infuse, but just remember to discard them before serving. Any leftover compote can be stored in the fridge for up to 1 week.

SWEET POTATO + KALE LATKES WITH POACHED EGGS SERVES 4

When I was cooking in cafés, the breakfast shift was always my favorite. This is the most "café-style" breakfast recipe in this book and one that I simply couldn't leave out. Lots of people get nervous at the idea of poaching eggs, but there's really no need: simmering water, a touch of vinegar to help congeal the whites, a swirl of water to centralize the yolk, gentle heat, and a good drain afterwards and, as Gordon Ramsay would say, "done."

1¼ pounds (600 g) orange (Beauregard) sweet potato, peeled + grated (see NOTE)

1 teaspoon sea salt

2 large kale leaves, stems removed + leaves finely chopped

1 spring onion, thinly sliced

2 large free-range eggs, lightly beaten

2 tablespoons chopped flat-leaf parsley

Olive oil or ghee

1 teaspoon cider vinegar

4–8 large free-range eggs (one or two per person, depending on how hungry you are)

Your favorite tomato chutney, to serve

+ Preheat oven to 250°F (120°C). Place sweet potato and salt in a bowl and mix well. Set aside for 10 minutes. Pick up handfuls of sweet potato and squeeze as hard as you can to remove all the excess liquid, then transfer to a clean bowl. Add kale, spring onion, eggs, and parsley and season with a few turns of your pepper mill.

+ Heat a couple of tablespoons of olive oil or ghee in a frying pan over medium-high heat. Add little handfuls (approx. ¼ cup) of mixture to the pan. I tend to squeeze them together as much as I can before placing them into the pan and then flatten them with a metal spatula, but they don't need to be perfect circles. Cook for 2–3 minutes or until golden on the underside, before flipping them over and cooking for another minute or two. Transfer to a paper towel–lined plate and pop into the oven to keep warm. Repeat with the remaining mixture. You should get 12 medium latkes (3 per person).

+ Fill a medium saucepan with at least 2 inches of water, add the cider vinegar, and bring to a boil. Reduce the heat to a simmer, create a whirlpool in the water with a large metal spoon, and crack 2–4 eggs into the pan at a time. Simmer for 3–4 minutes, depending on how well done you like your eggs. Lift each out with a large metal slotted spoon. Drain on a clean tea towel or paper towel.

+ To serve, place three latkes on each plate and top with one or two poached eggs. Season with a sprinkle of sea salt and freshly ground black pepper and place a generous dollop of tomato chutney on the side.

NOTE: Red (Owairaka) or golden (Toka toka) sweet potato, two favorite New Zealand varieties, can be used in place of orange, but I just love the color and sweetness of the Beauregard. Experiment with varieties you find in season at your local markets.

ROASTED RHUBARB WITH ORANGE YOGURT SERVES 4

Rhubarb is one of those foods I didn't understand as a child—to me it was all just string and mush, but maybe that was just how my mum used to cook the hell out of it in her little iron pot! Roasting it not only keeps it from turning stringy, but also intensifies the flavor and beautiful color. For a change, I sometimes leave out the rose water and add a few sprigs of rosemary during roasting. To make this into a more substantial breakfast, try topping these parfaits with muesli or puffed brown rice or millet.

roasted rhubarb

6 stalks (approx. 10 ounces) rhubarb, trimmed + cut into 2-inch lengths

⅓ cup (65 g) unrefined raw sugar

Juice of 1 orange

1 teaspoon rose water (optional)

orange yogurt

3 cups (750 g) natural plain yogurt or homemade labneh (page 222)

Finely grated zest of 1 orange

Honey or brown rice syrup, to taste

¼ cup (40 g) chopped pistachios, to serve

+ Preheat oven to 350°F (180°C). Mix together rhubarb, sugar, and orange juice, transfer to a rimmed baking sheet lined with parchment paper and spread out in a single layer. Roast for 15–18 minutes or until just tender but not mushy. Remove from the oven, sprinkle with rose water, and set aside to cool.

+ Meanwhile, mix together yogurt and orange zest and sweeten to taste with honey or syrup. (I don't usually sweeten mine as I find the syrup from the rhubarb is more than sweet enough.)

+ To serve, alternate layers of orange yogurt and roasted rhubarb (with syrup) into glasses, finishing with a good dollop of yogurt and a sprinkle of chopped pistachios. Or stop being a fancy pants and just plop it all into a bowl and enjoy...

BREAKFAST SMOOTHIE MAKES APPROX. 4 CUPS (1 LITER)

This is how I make my smoothies on days when I can't be bothered to strain the pulp to make almond milk! I don't mind a little added texture in my smoothies, so I just blend the whole soaked nuts with everything else and enjoy. If you don't like quite so much "roughness" in your morning smoothie, use blanched almonds instead of whole raw ones. To add extra oomph, I often add a few tablespoons of natural pea protein powder and a couple of tablespoons of soaked chia seeds.

1 cup (150 g) whole raw almonds, soaked overnight in cold water

2 peeled frozen bananas, chopped into chunks (see NOTE)

1 tablespoon virgin coconut oil (melted, if solid)

2–3 tablespoons honey, pure maple or brown rice syrup, to taste

2 cups (500 ml) water

Natural pea protein powder, optional

Soaked chia seeds (see NOTE), optional

+ Drain almonds, rinse under cold water, and drain again. Place in a blender with remaining ingredients and 2 cups (500 ml) water and blend on high for 1–2 minutes or until thick and creamy. Serve immediately.

NOTE: My freezer is always stocked with ripe bananas that I buy whenever I see them cheap. I use them for making banana berry ice cream (page 182) and smoothies. Simply peel overripe bananas and freeze whole on a tray before transferring to ziplock bags. If they are really nice and ripe, they will be easy to chop or break into chunks even when frozen.

NOTE: Chia seeds are able to absorb and hold an amazing amount of liquid. This is perfect for dishes such as chia pudding (page 54) where their gelling properties are used to your advantage. However, if you suffer at all from constipation, you need to soak the seeds in water or milk for at least 30 minutes before consuming. Otherwise those seeds will go on absorbing liquid in your gut, leaving you ... er ... blocked up. I usually go with the rule: 1 tablespoon chia seeds to 3 tablespoons water or almond milk. Give them a good stir for the first minute to prevent lumps from forming, set aside for 5 minutes, stir again, and set aside for 30 minutes before eating or adding to smoothies. Soaked chia seeds will keep in a glass jar in the fridge for up to 3 days.

GREEN SMOOTHIE MAKES APPROX. 4 CUPS (1 LITER)

In summertime, when mangoes are falling off the trees in our yard, this is the smoothie the kids request for breakfast. With a few handfuls of Swiss chard from the garden (or bought spinach) this can be whipped up in no time, making it one of the greatest ways I know to get the goodness of greens into kids (and adults too). The freshly squeezed orange juice helps the absorption of iron from the chard.

1 large ripe mango, chopped, or 1 cup chopped fresh pineapple

1 cup (250 ml) freshly squeezed orange juice

4–6 Swiss chard leaves, hard stems removed, leaves roughly chopped

2 peeled frozen bananas, chopped into chunks (see NOTE)

1 tablespoon virgin coconut oil, melted

+ Put everything in a blender—if you have a regular blender like I do (not a Vitamix), it's easier on the blender if you layer the softest ingredients and liquids first, in the order I've listed them. Add the coconut oil at the very end and blend immediately, or it will solidify again with all that frozen banana in there. Blend on high for 1 minute or until bright green, smooth, and creamy. Serve immediately.

NOTE: My freezer is always stocked with ripe bananas that I buy whenever I see them cheap. I use them for making banana berry ice cream (page 182) and smoothies. Simply peel overripe bananas and freeze whole on a tray before transferring to ziplock bags. If they are really nice and ripe, they will be easy to chop or break into chunks even when frozen.

EGGY BAKED TORTILLA CUPS MAKES 6

Corn tortillas make the perfect base for this simple but flavorsome frittata mix. It may take a few attempts to get the softened tortillas into the bowls/tins without tearing them, but even if they do have a few small holes they will still be delicious. This is a great way to use up leftover cooked potatoes, or use sweet potato or pumpkin if that's what you have. You can make the onion mixture and keep it for up to 1 week in a glass jar or container in the fridge. Do make sure you grease your bowls/tins well and remember the little round of parchment paper in the bottom. I've learned that runaway egg mixture and corn tortillas, when combined with heat, will stick to the bowls like glue! You have been warned . . .

3 medium potatoes,
  peeled + sliced into
  ½-inch rounds
3 tablespoons olive oil
2 red onions, finely sliced
4 garlic cloves, finely
  chopped
2 teaspoons paprika
2 tablespoons red wine
  vinegar
6 white corn tortillas
8 large free-range eggs,
  beaten well
2 tablespoons roughly
  chopped cilantro
  + extra leaves, to serve
tomato chutney, to serve,
  optional

+ Preheat oven to 350°F (180°C). Grease six 1-cup (250 ml) ovenproof bowls or large muffin tins and place a small round of parchment paper into the bottom of each. If using bowls, place on a baking sheet.

+ Pop potato slices into a saucepan, add a good pinch of salt, and cover with cold water. Bring to a boil and cook for 8–10 minutes or until just tender. Drain well.

+ Heat a frying pan over medium heat. Add olive oil, onions, and garlic. Cook, stirring often, for 8–10 minutes or until very soft. Add paprika and cook for 30 seconds before adding red wine vinegar, cooking until evaporated. Season well with sea salt and freshly ground black pepper.

+ Lay tortillas onto two baking sheets and warm in the oven for 45–60 seconds or until just softened. Working quickly, gently press a tortilla into each bowl or muffin tin. You will need to overlap it a little and try not to press down too hard on the bottom or you will tear it. If you feel more comfortable, just heat and line one bowl at a time.

+ Place alternating layers of potato and onion mixture into each tortilla cup. Season the beaten eggs well with salt and freshly ground black pepper and then pour into each cup, trying your best to keep the mixture in the cup without too much of it running down the side of the tortilla. Sprinkle with cilantro and bake for 20–25 minutes or until crispy on the outside and cooked through in the middle. Remove from the oven and set aside for 5 minutes. Run a knife around the edge of each cup to loosen and then gently tip out each one.

+ Serve immediately or at room temperature, scattered with extra cilantro leaves and tomato chutney on the side. I've also successfully reheated leftover tortilla cups in the oven on low heat the following day.

ORANGE CINNAMON CHIA PUDDING SERVES 3–4

Chia seeds are awesome little things to add into your diet: not only are they high in omega-3s and omega-6s, but also protein, iron, and calcium. While the boys in my family don't get the whole chia pudding thing, Ada and I can't get enough of it. And any excuse to eat pudding for breakfast has to be good, right? This can be kept covered in the fridge for up to 3 days (although it certainly wouldn't last that long in my house with Ada around).

½ cup (70 g) chia seeds, black or white, it doesn't matter

2 cups (500 ml) vanilla cashew or almond milk (preferably homemade, page 162)

2 tablespoons pure maple or brown rice syrup, to taste

1½ teaspoons ground cinnamon

1 teaspoon finely grated orange zest

Fresh fruit and chopped nuts, for serving

+ Combine all the ingredients in a bowl, stirring for the first minute to prevent lumps forming. Leave for 5 minutes, stir again, and then set aside at room temperature for 30 minutes (or store in a covered container in the fridge overnight for the following day). Stir well and serve with fresh fruit and chopped nuts.

JUICE, THREE WAYS SERVES 1

In summer the juicer lives out on the counter to try to inspire and remind me to get to it every morning! The kids love helping out with juicing: not only the drinking bit (which they're always keen on) but the pushing-through-the-chute bit, too. There's something about all that noise and excitement that has them scrambling to pull their chairs over to the counter to help.

Below are three of my favorite juice combinations to date. These are the ratios I would use for myself, but juicing really is a matter of personal taste. So, feel free to chop and change my suggestions as much as you like.

tangelo, carrot + ginger

3 tangelos, peeled + cut into small pieces

3 large carrots, cut into small pieces

1 small knob fresh ginger

beet, apple + fennel

3 apples, cut into small pieces

1 beet, cut into small pieces

1 fennel bulb, cut into small pieces

¼ lemon, peeled

green juice

2 apples, cut into small pieces

⅓ telegraph cucumber, cut into small pieces

2–4 kale, Swiss chard, or a big handful of spinach, stalks discarded

Small handful of flat-leaf parsley

¼ lemon, peeled

tangelo, carrot + ginger

✛ Run all of the ingredients through your juicer and enjoy. I love the flavor and juiciness of tangelos, but oranges or mandarins can be used in their place. Pink grapefruit makes for a lovely variation too.

beet, apple + fennel

✛ Run all of the ingredients through your juicer and enjoy. Not a fan of fennel or can't get your hands on any? No worries: a few celery stalks are a great substitute, in which case a touch of ginger is also nice.

green juice

✛ Run all the ingredients through your juicer and enjoy. This one will make you feel invincible!

BLUEBERRY + BANANA BREAKFAST MUFFINS MAKES 12

It's no secret that I prefer sweet over savory first thing in the morning, but that doesn't mean I want a full sugar hit either. These moist muffins are sweetened by nothing more than overripe bananas and a touch of pure maple syrup. Other than being high in protein (which is what I always look for in a good breakfast), they make me happy because they can be cooked the night before—a perfect on-the-go breakfast to grab as you run out the door.

¾ cup mashed banana (approx. 2 very over-ripe bananas)

3 large free-range eggs

2 tablespoons pure maple syrup

1 teaspoon apple cider vinegar

1 teaspoon vanilla extract

Finely grated zest of 1 lemon

1½ cups (165 g) ground almonds

½ teaspoon gluten-free baking powder

½ teaspoon baking soda

1 cup (125 g) blueberries, fresh or frozen

½ banana, peeled + sliced

+ Preheat oven to 350°F (180°C). Line a 12-hole ⅓ cup (80 ml) muffin tin with paper liners. Don't skip this step or these muffins will be forever stuck in your tin!

+ Whisk together mashed banana, eggs, maple syrup, cider vinegar, vanilla, and lemon zest until smooth. Add ground almonds and sift in the baking powder, soda, and a pinch of fine sea salt. Mix until just combined before gently folding in blueberries (if using frozen, do not defrost before using).

+ Spoon into tin, top each one with a few slices of banana, and bake for 20–25 minutes or until a skewer inserted into the center comes out clean. Remove from the oven and set aside for 5 minutes before transferring the lined muffins to a wire rack to cool completely. Leave for 1–2 hours before eating (otherwise the paper liners have an annoying tendency to stick to the muffins!) or store in an airtight container for up to 3 days.

SMALL PLATES

We eat very simply for lunch most days. I generally grab leftovers from dinner the night before, sometimes reheated (but mostly just lazily straight from the fridge), or I fix a quick and easy salad for myself.

I didn't think this chapter would be very exciting if it consisted of my usual lunchtime fare. Instead you will find all manner of savory recipes that fit under the banner of small (savory) plates. Some, such as lentil tapenade with chickpea crackers, are perfect alongside drinks; savory muffins are great to pack for lunch on the go with a thermos of soup; while rice paper rolls are just the thing for a quick, light meal at the end of a long day.

SWEETCORN + BASIL FRITTERS   MAKES 12 FRITTERS

Corn fritters were always one of my favorite foods as a child and they're still one of the first things I think to make when I'm in a hurry. They are great with eggs in the morning, can be eaten straight up for a quick snack or light lunch, and, paired with minty boiled new potatoes and a fresh garden salad, make a perfect alfresco summer dinner. Making fritters with fresh corn is the best, but I also make these in the winter with frozen, locally grown corn kernels. I swap a handful of chopped flat-leaf parsley for the basil when it's out of season.

2 fresh corncobs, husks removed (or 2 cups frozen corn kernels)

⅔ cup (75 g) chickpea (chana or besan) flour

⅓ cup (35 g) tapioca or gluten-free organic cornstarch

2 teaspoons baking powder

½ teaspoon sea salt

1 large free-range egg, separated

½ cup (125 ml) water

¼ cup roughly chopped basil leaves

2 tablespoons finely chopped chives

Olive oil or ghee

+ Place corn in a large saucepan of salted water, bring to a boil, and cook until tender. Super-fresh corn will be done in around 5 minutes while older cobs can take up to 10 minutes. (I was always taught that corn is cooked when you can smell it throughout the room.) Remove from the heat, drain, and set aside until cool enough to handle, then shave corn kernels off the cob with a sharp knife. If you are using frozen corn kernels, plunge into boiling water for a few minutes, then drain before using.

+ Sift flour, cornstarch, and baking powder into a bowl and add sea salt and a few pinches of freshly ground black pepper. Combine egg yolk and ½ cup (125 ml) cold water and add to the flour mixture, whisking to form a smooth, thin batter. Add corn, basil, and chives and mix to combine. Cover and set aside on the counter for at least 10 minutes and up to 1 hour.

+ When ready to cook, whisk the egg white in a clean bowl until stiff peaks form. Fold 1–2 tablespoons of egg white into the batter to loosen the mixture before gently folding in the rest with a large metal spoon. Heat 2–3 tablespoons of oil or ghee in a heavy-bottomed frying pan over medium heat and cook large spoonfuls of batter for 2–3 minutes or until bubbles show on the top and the underside is golden. Flip fritters over with a wide metal spatula and cook for a few minutes longer until golden and cooked through. Repeat until all the batter is cooked. Drain fritters on paper towels and sprinkle with extra sea salt to serve.

SNOW PEA + AVOCADO NOODLE SALAD WITH SOY GINGER DRESSING
SERVES 2–3 AS A LIGHT MEAL OR MORE AS A SIDE DISH

This is a quick salad version of my rice paper rolls (page 72). It's a great way for me to overdose on the flavors I love so much, without having to muck around with any rolling. Any rice noodle works here: I sometimes use thin round rice noodles that take a little longer to cook, or you can use flat rice noodles, either thin or thick. And I always remove the inner string from the snow pea: snap off the leafy tip, pulling toward the inside of the pea, and then give a quick downward tug.

1 large handful (approx. 3½ ounces) of snow peas, trimmed

8-ounce (185 g) package dried flat rice noodles

1 ripe avocado, cut into bite-sized chunks

1 cup loosely packed mint leaves, roughly torn

½ cup loosely packed cilantro leaves, roughly torn

½ cup loosely packed Thai basil leaves, roughly torn, optional

1 spring onion, finely sliced

¼ cup (30 g) lightly toasted cashews or peanuts

½ cup fried shallots (see NOTE)

Sliced bird's eye chili, to serve, optional

soy ginger dressing

1 garlic clove, finely chopped

¼ teaspoon fine sea salt

2 tablespoons finely grated ginger

1 long red chili (cayenne or Thai), deseeded + finely chopped

1 tablespoon unrefined raw sugar or grated pure palm sugar

Finely grated zest + juice of 1 lemon

¼ cup (60 ml) gluten-free soy sauce

+ Bring a large saucepan of salted water to a boil and cook snow peas for 45–60 seconds until just tender but still a lovely bright green; lift out and transfer to a bowl of iced water. When the snow peas are cold, drain and slice finely. Bring the saucepan of water back to a boil and add rice noodles, stirring to separate. Cook for 4–5 minutes until just tender (depending on type and thickness of your noodles). Tip into a colander and rinse under cold water to stop the cooking. Drain well.

+ To make soy ginger dressing, sprinkle garlic with salt and use the side of your knife to mash it to a paste. Transfer to a bowl. Place the grated ginger into your hand, hold it over the bowl and squeeze to extract as much of the ginger juice as you can. Discard the pulp. Add remaining dressing ingredients and taste: if your lemons are ultra-tart, you may want to add a touch more sugar. Not salty enough? Add a touch more soy or a pinch of salt. You're looking for a perfect balance of salty, sweet, sour, and hot. You can also make the dressing with a mortar and pestle.

+ Mix noodles with remaining salad ingredients, tossing well. Spoon over enough dressing to coat, mix, and serve. Store any leftover dressing in a glass jar in the fridge. If you are making this in advance, keep all the components separate until just before serving, or the noodles will soak up all that lovely dressing.

NOTE: You can buy fried shallots at your local Asian grocer, but they are really easy to make at home. Just thinly slice a couple of red Asian shallots and fry in 2 tablespoons olive oil until deep golden and slightly crispy, using a wooden spoon to break up the rings. Remove from the heat and lay in a single layer on a piece of paper towel to cool and crisp up further.

LENTIL TAPENADE WITH CHICKPEA CRACKERS

SERVES 4–6 (MAKES 3 CUPS TAPENADE OR TOPS 24 SMALL CRACKERS)

This tapenade is salty and sour from the olives and lemon juice, while the lentils add a lovely earthiness and protein boost. Both the tapenade and crackers can be prepared well in advance, and you could also serve with veggie sticks or cheese. Puy lentils bring deep color and firmness, but you can use regular brown lentils, too. Lentils don't require soaking overnight and can be cooked from dried; however, when I remember, I prefer to soak them—it makes them easier to digest and much quicker to cook.

1 cup (210 g) Puy-style lentils, rinsed

3 garlic cloves, peeled but left whole

¼ teaspoon freshly ground black pepper

1 bay leaf, fresh or dried

1¼ cups (215 g) pitted kalamata olives

3 tablespoons capers, drained

3 tablespoons lemon juice, or to taste

3 tablespoons extra-virgin olive oil, or to taste

chickpea crackers

¾ cup (135 g) dried chickpeas, soaked in plenty of cold water overnight, or 15-ounce (400 g) can cooked chickpeas, rinsed well, or 1½ cups leftover cooked chickpeas

½ cup (50 g) tapioca flour or gluten-free organic cornstarch

¼ cup (30 g) lightly toasted sesame seeds

½ teaspoon fine sea salt

½ teaspoon freshly ground black pepper

2 tablespoons extra-virgin olive oil

+ To make chickpea crackers, drain soaked chickpeas, rinse well, and put in a saucepan. Cover with plenty of cold water and bring to a boil. Reduce heat and simmer for 25–35 minutes or until tender but not falling apart. Drain well and set aside to cool. Blend in a food processor until finely ground and then transfer to a bowl. Add tapioca flour, sesame seeds, salt, pepper, and olive oil. Use your hands to mix to a soft dough. Turn out onto a lightly rice-floured board and knead a few times to bring dough together. Shape into a flat disc, cover, and chill in the fridge for 30 minutes.

+ Preheat oven to 350°F (180°C). Roll out dough between two sheets of lightly rice-floured parchment paper to about ⅛" thick and score dough into shapes. Alternatively, take small pieces of dough and roll out into long rustic shapes (as shown in the photo). Remove the top layer of parchment paper and use the bottom layer to transfer the whole lot to a baking sheet. Bake for 18–20 minutes until crisp and lightly golden around the edges. Remove from oven and cool on the tray for 5 minutes before transferring to a wire rack to cool completely. If you've scored them, snap the crackers apart when cold. They are best eaten on day of baking, but they will store in an airtight container for 2–3 days.

+ To make the lentil tapenade, place lentils into a saucepan with the garlic, pepper, and bay leaf. Cover with plenty of cold water, bring to a boil, then reduce to a simmer and cook for 25–30 minutes or until tender (time will vary depending on freshness of your lentils). Drain well and discard bay leaf.

+ Place lentils, olives, capers, lemon juice, and oil in a food processor and pulse until nearly smooth (I like a little chunkiness to my tapenade). Season with sea salt and freshly ground black pepper, if needed. Serve with chickpea crackers or store in a covered container in the fridge for up to 4 days.

MUNG BEAN PANCAKES WITH SATAY VEGETABLES MAKES 10 PANCAKES

When I worked as a pastry chef, sweet stuff was often the only thing I ate all day. When you're too busy to stop and eat a real meal, you tend to just nibble what's in front of you, which is not so good when you're on desserts! On the counter behind me worked my two Filipino friends, and they would sneak me a few of whatever savory vegetarian dishes they were making that day. My favorite of all the contraband foods were little mung bean pancakes, filled with crisp, finely sliced vegetables, all bound together with a tangy lime-kissed satay sauce. If you own a mandoline, use it here for finely shredding the carrot and cabbages for the filling.

¼ cup (50 g) whole dried mung beans, soaked overnight in plenty of water
1¼ cups (310 ml) coconut milk
3 large free-range eggs
1 cup (125 g) white rice flour
½ teaspoon turmeric powder
½ teaspoon fine sea salt
Olive oil

satay sauce
2 tablespoons olive oil
1 onion, finely diced
2 garlic cloves, finely chopped
1 tablespoon finely grated ginger
2 bird's eye chilies, finely chopped
1 teaspoon curry powder
¾ cup (185 g) natural peanut butter (chunky or smooth)
¼ cup (65 g) coconut sugar (grated if in solid block form), or use muscovado sugar
¼ cup (60 ml) freshly squeezed lime (or lemon) juice
3 tablespoons (45 ml) gluten-free soy sauce
½ cup (125 ml) water
1–2 tablespoons rice vinegar, or to taste

Small handful of snow peas, trimmed + sliced thinly (see NOTE)
1 small carrot, sliced into thin matchsticks
½ cup finely shredded red cabbage
½ cup finely shredded cabbage
Small handful of mung bean sprouts
¼ cup finely shredded mint leaves
¼ cup finely chopped cilantro
¼ cup (30 g) unsalted natural roasted peanuts, roughly chopped
2 spring onions, thinly sliced
1–2 limes
Finely sliced red chili + lime wedges, to serve

+ Drain mung beans and place in blender with the coconut milk. Blend on high for 45–60 seconds or until a paste forms with just little green flecks of mung bean skin showing. Add eggs, rice flour, turmeric, and salt. Blend on high for another 20–30 seconds, stopping to scrape down the side of the carafe and give it one more quick blitz until the batter is relatively smooth.

+ Pour into a fine sieve over a clean bowl and use a metal spoon to press out any lumps and mung bean skins as the mixture goes through (you will have about 1 tablespoon bean skins left in the sieve; discard these). Be sure you scrape the underside of the sieve to catch all the good bits there too. Cover and set aside. The batter can be prepared a few hours beforehand or even kept in the fridge overnight (although you may need to thin it down a little the next day).

+ To make satay sauce, heat oil in a heavy-bottomed saucepan over medium heat. Add onion and cook, stirring, for 2–3 minutes until tender but not colored. Add garlic, ginger, chili, and curry powder and cook for another 1–2 minutes until fragrant. Remove from heat, add peanut butter, sugar, lime juice, soy sauce, and ½ cup (125 ml) cold water. Return to the heat and bring to a simmer, stirring with a wooden spoon to dissolve the peanut butter. Add 1–2 tablespoons rice vinegar—just enough to make it sing—season with sea salt and freshly ground black pepper and stir in more cold water

if needed, thinning it down to sauce consistency. Simmer for 5–8 minutes to develop the flavors, then remove from the heat. If not needed immediately, cool and store in a covered container in the fridge for up to 1 week. You may need to add a touch of water before serving as it will thicken up in the fridge.

+ In a large bowl combine sliced snow peas, carrot, cabbages, mung bean shoots, herbs, peanuts, and spring onion. Mix well.

+ Heat an 8-inch frying pan or wok over medium-high heat, add the teeniest bit of olive oil, and swirl the pan around to coat evenly (tip out any excess if you need to). Pour in enough batter to just cover the bottom (approx. ¼ cup), tilting the pan to evenly coat with a thin layer of batter as you would for regular crepes. Cook for 30–45 seconds or until the underside is golden. Flip over with a wide metal spatula and cook for another 10–15 seconds or until cooked through. Remove from the pan and transfer to a plate or wire cooling rack. Repeat with remaining batter, stacking pancakes on top of each other and covering with a clean tea towel.

+ To serve, squeeze the juice of 1–2 limes over the shredded vegetables and mix it all up. Smear a generous dollop of satay sauce down the center of each pancake, top with a handful of shredded vegetables, and a few slices of chili if you like more heat, fold in the ends, and roll up neatly. Serve with lime wedges.

NOTE: I always remove the inner string from my snow peas before using. Simply snap off the leafy tip, pulling it toward the inside of the pea. A quick downward tug should take care of the rest.

ROASTED SQUASH, SWEET POTATO + CILANTRO SOUP SERVES 4

Whenever I buy a large bunch of cilantro and only use the leaves in a recipe, I finely chop the stems and roots, pop them into a ziplock bag and freeze for later. This recipe is one of those "laters." It's only the flavor of the cilantro stems that is needed here to boost the roasted vegetables before they're blended into a smooth creamy soup.

2 pounds butternut squash, seeded, peeled + chopped into 1½-inch chunks

1 pound kumara (sweet potato), peeled + cut into 1½-inch chunks

1 large onion, cut into 8 wedges

4 garlic cloves, peeled + left whole

½ cup finely chopped cilantro stalks

2 teaspoons whole cumin seeds

3 tablespoons virgin coconut oil, melted

4–5 cups (1–1.25 liters) vegetable stock (page 236)

Coconut milk, to serve

+ Preheat oven to 375°F (190°C). Combine squash, sweet potato, onion, garlic, cilantro stalks, cumin seeds, and coconut oil in a large bowl. Season generously with sea salt and black pepper. Spread in a single layer in a large deep roasting pan and roast for 30–35 minutes, turning every 15 minutes until golden and tender. Transfer to a blender and blend in batches, adding the stock bit by bit, until smooth. (Alternatively, put the lot in a large saucepan and blend until smooth with a stick blender.) Transfer to a large saucepan over medium heat and bring up to a simmer before serving, drizzled with a little coconut milk and with plenty of hot buttered toast on the side.

AVOCADO + CASHEW RICE PAPER ROLLS SERVES 4–6

It seems that we Westerners get a few things wrong when it comes to making rice paper rolls. If I remember correctly, this was one of the first things my mother-in-law said when we met (right after: "Wow, she's tall"). Most of us are led to believe (because it's even printed on the back of the pack) that rice paper wrappers have to be soaked in hot water for 1–2 minutes until supersoft, then dried on a clean tea towel . . . Do this and the wrapper becomes one of the most fragile things around. There is an easier way. You don't need to use boiling water. I pour boiling water into bowls and then add some cold water to cool it down. Now dip your wrapper into the water for a few seconds, just long enough to wet it, but not long enough to soften it. Transfer to a large flat plate and fill with whatever fillings you like. By the time you have placed all your fillings, the rice paper will have softened perfectly and dried off naturally. Roll up and enjoy.

An even easier way (for the cook!) is to eat these in traditional Vietnamese style. Set the table with plates of fillings, small bowls of dipping sauce and a couple of water bowls for dipping the wrappers. Each person can then make their own rolls, instead of one of us being in the kitchen making the whole lot.

If you want to make these in advance, roll them up, place on a large platter (or in a lidded container), and cover with a damp tea towel to prevent the papers from drying out. They will keep like this for 2–3 hours at room temperature (but not the fridge, or they'll dry out). You could also serve these with the soy dipping sauce from my bánh xèo recipe (page 126).

Two 50 g packages vermicelli noodles
12½ ounces (350 g) firm tofu
Olive oil
2 teaspoons gluten-free soy sauce
½ teaspoon sesame oil
2 thinly sliced ripe avocados, lettuce leaves, cucumber matchsticks, mung bean sprouts + mint leaves, to serve
1½ cups (185 g) lightly toasted cashews or peanuts, roughly chopped
1 package large (9-inch) round Vietnamese rice paper wrappers

hot + sour sauce
¼ cup (60 ml) fresh lime or lemon juice
2–3 tablespoons finely grated pure palm sugar or unrefined raw sugar
1 bird's eye chili, finely chopped (deseeded, if you want to reduce heat)

hoisin dipping sauce
Gluten-free hoisin sauce
Lime juice or hot water, to thin
Finely chopped bird's eye chili, optional

+ Put vermicelli in a bowl, cover with boiling water, and let it soften for 10 minutes. Drain well.

+ Rinse tofu, pat dry on paper towels, and cut into ⅓-inch slices. Heat a large frying pan over medium-high heat, add a touch of olive oil, and panfry tofu for 3–4 minutes on either side, or until golden and crisp. Drizzle with soy sauce and sesame oil and season with salt and pepper. Mix well, then remove from the heat. Once cool enough to handle, slice each piece of tofu into long, thin pieces.

+ Arrange avocado, lettuce, cucumber, mung bean sprouts, mint leaves, and tofu onto plates and place in the center of the table, along with a bowl of cashews or peanuts and the drained vermicelli.

+ To make the hot + sour sauce, combine all ingredients in a bowl, stirring to dissolve the sugar. To make the hoisin sauce, place as much hoisin as required into a small bowl and thin with lime juice to reach a good dipping sauce consistency. Add the chili. (This is how I make it for myself; for the children, I thin down with hot water and leave out the chili.)

(continued)

+ When ready to eat, place a few large shallow bowls of hot water on table. People can dip their own wrappers in the water (just long enough to soften a little), then lay their filling ingredients in a neat pile in the center of the wrapper. To roll up, simply pull the bottom half of the paper up to meet the top, fold in both sides, and then roll tightly toward the top of your plate. Serve dipped in plenty of sauce and replenish lettuce, cucumber, mung bean sprouts, or mint as needed. You're likely to have leftover rice paper wrappers so just store them for next time.

CORN, CILANTRO + FETA MUFFINS MAKES 10

These savory muffins are packed with flavor and dotted with a generous amount of corn, cilantro, and salty feta cheese. They are perfect for a mid-morning snack or with a bowl of hot soup. If you want to make them dairy-free, simply omit the feta and use olive oil in place of butter/ghee. These are best eaten on the day they're baked, but can be stored in an airtight container for 2–3 days.

½ cup (55 g) ground almonds

⅓ cup (45 g) fine polenta

½ cup (70 g) fine brown rice flour

2 tablespoons tapioca flour or gluten-free organic cornstarch

2 teaspoons gluten-free baking powder

½ teaspoon fine sea salt

1 cup corn kernels, shaved from 1 cob cooked corn (following first step on page 62), or frozen kernels

½ cup cilantro leaves and tender stems, roughly chopped

1 spring onion, finely sliced, or a small handful of finely chopped chives

1 cup (approx. 100 g) crumbled feta cheese

¼ cup (60 ml) melted ghee/butter or olive oil

2 large free-range eggs

¾ cup (185 ml) rice or almond milk

+ Preheat oven to 350°F (180°C). Line a 10-hole ⅓ cup (80 ml) muffin tin with paper liners.

+ Place ground almonds and polenta in a bowl and sift in brown rice flour, tapioca flour, and baking powder. Add salt and a good pinch freshly ground black pepper and whisk to combine. Add corn (if using frozen, don't defrost first), cilantro, spring onion, and two-thirds of the feta.

+ In another bowl whisk ghee/butter or oil, eggs, and milk until smooth. Pour into flour mixture and stir until just combined. Spoon evenly into muffin tin, scatter with rest of the feta, and bake for 25 minutes or until risen, golden, and a skewer inserted into the center comes out clean. Set aside for 5 minutes, before transferring muffins to a wire rack to cool.

CARROT, CUMIN + RED LENTIL SOUP WITH CILANTRO CASHEW PESTO
SERVES 4–6

This is one of my favorite soups to make, perhaps because it uses ingredients that I always have on hand. Budget-friendly carrots, fragrant cumin, and earthy red lentils form the base, and a spoonful of my favorite pesto tops it off. This is made with toasted cashews and a good dollop of white miso to give the illusion of Parmesan cheese. White miso, also known as shiromiso, is a Japanese fermented soybean paste that's light brown in color and has a slightly sweet and salty flavor. I buy my paste in small tubs from my local Asian grocer and keep it in the fridge once opened. I recommend you avoid the single-serving sachets as they sometimes have MSG added to them. White miso is very mild in flavor, compared to most other types, and is often fermented with rice, not barley, meaning it is also gluten-free. Do check the labels carefully though to ensure no gluten is present if you are celiac or very sensitive to gluten. To make this dairy-free (and consequently vegan) use virgin coconut oil, not ghee.

2 tablespoons ghee or virgin coconut oil

2 onions, finely diced

3 garlic cloves, finely chopped

2 teaspoons cumin seeds, lightly toasted + finely ground

1 cup (180 g) red lentils, rinsed

3 large carrots, grated

8 cups (2 liters) vegetable stock (page 236)

2 teaspoons fine sea salt, or to taste

Juice of ½ lemon

cilantro cashew pesto

3 cups (70 g) loosely packed, roughly chopped cilantro leaves + tender stalks

½ cup (60 g) lightly toasted cashews

3 tablespoons extra-virgin olive oil

1 long green chili, roughly chopped (deseeded, if you prefer)

1 garlic clove, roughly chopped

2–3 teaspoons white (shiro) miso, or to taste

+ Melt ghee or oil in a large saucepan over medium heat. Add onion, garlic, and cumin and cook, stirring often, for 8–10 minutes or until very soft and golden brown. Add lentils, carrot, stock, and salt. Increase heat and bring to a boil, skimming off any foam that rises to the surface. Reduce to a simmer and cook for 25–30 minutes or until the lentils collapse and carrot is tender. Remove half of the soup and blend until smooth, then return to the pan (or, if you like a completely smooth soup, blitz the whole lot). Add lemon juice and season with sea salt and freshly ground black pepper. Serve hot with a dollop of cilantro cashew pesto on top to stir through, or spread the pesto over hot toast.

+ To make cilantro cashew pesto, place all of the ingredients in a blender or small food processor and blend until smooth, stopping to scrape down the side a few times. Season to taste with sea salt and black pepper.

KALE SLAW WITH HONEY MUSTARD MISO DRESSING SERVES 4–6

My family tolerates dairy in small amounts nowadays, but when we ate strictly dairy-free, one of the foods I most craved was feta. To me, most salads are incomplete without a little of its salty creamy goodness. So I came up with this miso-based dressing that gives the same depth of flavor. We love raw kale salads in our house, for the earthiness and texture the kale brings and also the happiness in knowing that we're all getting a good dose of vitamins and minerals. Kale is especially high in calcium, magnesium, and vitamins A, B6, C, and K.

If you don't have the specific ingredients listed below, feel free to ad-lib: it's the salty dressing and toasted sesame seeds that make this salad really special. (So much so that I've been known to eat just shredded cabbage mixed with the dressing and seeds to get my fix!)

2 large handfuls of curly kale or Tuscan kale (approx. 6–7 medium leaves), thick stems removed (see NOTE)

2 cups finely shredded white cabbage

2 cups finely shredded red cabbage

⅓ cup (40 g) lightly toasted sesame seeds

honey mustard miso dressing

3 tablespoons white (shiro) miso

1 tablespoon Dijon mustard

1 tablespoon honey

⅓ cup (80 ml) apple cider vinegar

½ cup (125 ml) extra-virgin olive oil

+ To make dressing, whisk white miso, mustard, and honey together until smooth. Add vinegar and whisk to combine. Slowly drizzle in olive oil, continuing to whisk, to form a thick emulsified dressing. Alternatively, blitz the whole lot in a mini food processor until creamy.

+ Roll up a few kale leaves at a time to form a long cigar. Using a sharp knife, finely shred the leaves and place in a large bowl with the remaining salad ingredients. Stir in just enough dressing to coat the salad, give it all a good mix and serve. Unlike lettuce-based salads, this keeps well for up to a few hours once dressed. (Store any leftover dressing in a glass jar in the fridge.)

NOTE: Most of the kale you see around is the curly leaf variety, also known as Scots kale, which you'll find in shades of both green and purple. If you're lucky, you'll come across cavolo nero, which also goes by the name of Tuscan kale, black cabbage, or Lacinato kale—its leaves are long and much more tender than the curly kale variety. Either will do for this recipe.

BUCKWHEAT TABOULI SERVES 4–6 AS A SIDE

Traditional tabouli is made using bulgur wheat—as we don't eat gluten, I make mine with cooked buckwheat instead. That might sound contradictory at first glance, but buckwheat is actually a gluten-free seed from a plant related to sorrel and rhubarb. Despite its name, it contains no wheat at all. I buy raw hulled buckwheat kernels, also known as groats and not to be confused with the toasted kernels known as kasha. I serve this on its own or with my sprouted chickpea falafel wraps (page 146).

1 cup (250 ml) water

½ cup (90 g) raw hulled buckwheat

3 cups flat-leaf parsley leaves and tender stems, finely chopped

1 cup mint leaves, finely chopped

2 large tomatoes, finely diced

1 small Lebanese cucumber or ⅓ medium telegraph cucumber, finely diced

3 spring onions, finely chopped

¼ cup (60 ml) lemon juice

3 tablespoons extra-virgin olive oil

1 tablespoon pomegranate molasses, optional

+ Bring 1 cup (250 ml) water and a pinch of sea salt to a boil in a saucepan. Add buckwheat, reduce heat to a simmer, cover and cook for 15–20 minutes or until water is absorbed and buckwheat tender. Remove the lid for the last few minutes of cooking to allow excess liquid to evaporate if needed. Remove from the heat, cover with the lid slightly ajar, and allow to cool. Fluff up with a fork. Combine buckwheat with parsley, mint, tomatoes, cucumber, and spring onion.

+ Whisk together lemon juice, olive oil, and pomegranate molasses. Season well with sea salt and freshly ground black pepper and pour over tabouli. Mix well, taste, and add more salt and black pepper if needed.

BROWN RICE SALAD WITH SPICE-ROASTED CARROTS, FETA + PINE NUTS

SERVES 4–6

Every dinner party my parents ever had featured my mother's famous brown rice salad. It was typical hippie vegetarian fare bound together in a dressing made from lemon juice, curry powder, and oil. I loved it then, and I still do. Here, I've taken inspiration from that salad and come up with my own version. Carrots are such an underrated vegetable—to some people they may seem a bit boring but, in their defense, they are very cheap, available year-round, and, when coated in spices and roasted until tender, they transform into something just a little bit posh. If pine nuts are out of your price range, toasted slivered or sliced almonds would do the trick here, too.

5 large carrots, peeled and cut into ½-inch thick diagonal slices

¼ cup finely chopped cilantro stalks

3 tablespoons olive oil

2 teaspoons cumin seeds

2 teaspoons coriander seeds, roughly ground

1 teaspoon paprika

½ teaspoon ground turmeric + ½ teaspoon, extra

1 cup (200 g) medium-grain brown rice, washed

1¾ cups (435 ml) water

½ cup (100 g) dried currants or organic raisins

2 tablespoons lightly toasted pine nuts

Large handful of cilantro leaves, roughly chopped

Large handful of flat-leaf parsley leaves, roughly chopped

Crumbled feta, to serve, optional

lemon dressing

¼ cup (60 ml) lemon juice

1 tablespoon apple cider vinegar

2 teaspoons honey

3 tablespoons extra-virgin olive oil

+ Preheat oven to 400°F (200°C). Place carrots, cilantro stalks, olive oil, cumin, coriander, paprika, and ½ teaspoon turmeric in a bowl, season well with sea salt and freshly ground black pepper, and mix well. Spread out in a single layer on a baking tray and roast for 25–30 minutes, turning often, until golden and tender. Set aside to cool.

+ Meanwhile, wash rice and drain well. Place rice, extra ½ teaspoon turmeric, and 1¾ cups (435 ml) water in a saucepan, cover with a tight-fitting lid, and bring to a boil. Reduce heat to lowest setting and simmer, covered, for 40–45 minutes or until water has been absorbed and rice is tender. (Alternatively, you can use a rice cooker.) Remove from heat, keeping the lid on, and leave for 10 minutes before removing the lid and cooling to room temperature.

+ To make lemon dressing, whisk together all ingredients. Pour over cooled rice (it may seem like too much, but the rice absorbs a lot of it), stir in the roasted carrots and any spices from the tray, currants, pine nuts, cilantro, and parsley. Adjust seasoning to taste. Serve with crumbled feta on top.

+ Any leftover salad will keep quite happily in the fridge until the following day, although you can add a little bit more salt and pepper and a squeeze of lemon juice to refresh the flavor.

QUINOA, ORANGE + ASPARAGUS SALAD
SERVES 4 AS A LIGHT MEAL OR MORE AS A SIDE

You know that moment at the start of spring, when the last of the winter citrus is still around, but fresh asparagus has just appeared? Well, that is the perfect time to make this wonderful salad. All out-of-season and imported citrus is coated in wax to help keep it fresh, so make sure you only pick or buy locally grown (or even better, organic) citrus when you're using the zest, so you don't end up with a plateful of chemical residue.

I haven't added it to the ingredients (I have to hold back from adding it to every dish), but a little crumbling of feta cheese over the top is also lovely here. And, by all means, roast or grill the asparagus if you prefer.

2 cups (500 ml) water
2 tablespoons olive oil
1 onion, finely diced
2 garlic cloves, finely chopped
1 tablespoon toasted sesame seeds
1 cup (185 g) quinoa, rinsed well
2 small bunches (approx. 14 ounces total) asparagus, woody ends trimmed, sliced into 1-inch lengths
Finely grated zest of ½ large orange
½ cup (85 g) toasted almonds, roughly chopped
1 cup loosely packed mint leaves, roughly torn

citrus dressing
Juice of ½ large orange
Juice of 1 lemon
2 teaspoons honey or unrefined raw sugar
3 tablespoons extra-virgin olive oil

+ Begin boiling about 2 cups (500 ml) of water in a kettle. Heat olive oil in a saucepan, add onion and garlic, and cook over medium heat for 2–3 minutes, stirring constantly until translucent. Add sesame seeds and quinoa and cook for 1–2 minutes, stirring often until lightly toasted. Add 1½ cups (375 ml) boiling water, reduce to a gentle simmer, cover pan, and cook for 10–12 minutes until all the water has been absorbed and quinoa is tender. Remove from heat. Leaving the lid on, set aside to steam for another 5 minutes before fluffing up with a fork. Cool to room temperature.

+ Meanwhile, blanch asparagus in a saucepan of salted boiling water for 1–2 minutes or until just tender. Drain and refresh in cold water.

+ To make citrus dressing, simmer orange and lemon juice in a small saucepan until reduced by half. Remove from the heat, add honey, and then pour in olive oil in a steady stream, whisking constantly to form a lovely emulsified dressing. Taste and season well with sea salt and freshly ground black pepper.

+ Transfer quinoa to a large bowl and stir in orange zest, almonds, mint, asparagus, and dressing. Toss well and adjust seasoning if needed.

EGGPLANT, TOMATO + FETA SALAD WITH POMEGRANATE DRESSING
SERVES 4–6

I was never a huge fan of eggplant until the last few years. (I've worked in too many cafés where it was sliced, doused in copious amounts of oil, and charred on the outside.) It wasn't until I started roasting it that I fell in love with its creamy (not oily) texture. Here the roasted eggplant pieces are free to soak up the sweet and tangy pomegranate dressing. I first made this salad when we had beautiful, slender, bright purple baby eggplants growing in our garden, not much longer than my finger. To keep this recipe achievable, I've used regular large eggplants here. This is a lovely salad to serve as a side, but if you want to make a meal of it, toss in a few cupfuls of cooked chickpeas.

2 medium eggplants
2–3 tablespoons olive oil
2 handfuls (250 g) cherry
   tomatoes, cut in half
100 g feta cheese,
   crumbled
Large handful of flat-leaf
   parsley leaves, roughly
   torn
Large handful of mint
   leaves, roughly torn

**pomegranate molasses
dressing**
1 teaspoon fennel seeds
1 small garlic clove,
   roughly chopped
¼ cup (60 ml) lemon juice
2 tablespoons honey
2 tablespoons
   pomegranate molasses
2 tablespoons extra-virgin
   olive oil

+ Preheat oven to 400°F (200°C). Line two baking sheets with parchment paper or grease well with olive oil. Slice eggplants into ½-inch rounds, then cut each round into quarters (or bite-sized pieces if you prefer). Transfer eggplant to baking sheets, drizzle with olive oil, and season well with sea salt and black pepper. Using your hands, mix well to evenly coat the eggplant in oil. Spread slices out in a single layer and roast for 15–20 minutes or until golden underneath. Flip each piece over and cook for another 10 minutes or until golden on both sides and tender. Remove from the oven and set pans aside to cool to room temperature.

+ Meanwhile, make the dressing by pounding the fennel seeds in a mortar and pestle (or spice/coffee grinder), adding the garlic and pounding until smooth. Add lemon juice, honey, and pomegranate molasses. Stir in olive oil in a steady stream, while mixing, to form a lovely emulsified dressing. Season to taste with sea salt and black pepper.

+ To serve, arrange alternate layers of eggplant, cherry tomatoes, crumbled feta, and herbs onto a serving platter. Drizzle with as much of the dressing as you like and serve. Any leftover dressing will store in a glass jar in the fridge for 1 week.

ARUGULA, PEAR + ALMOND SALAD WITH CHIVE DRESSING
SERVES 4 AS A SIDE

I eat a huge bowlful of salad each and every day. Mostly it's just a mishmash of whatever vegetables I have lying around in my fridge with a little feta and my go-to miso dressing. But there are certain times of the year when a bunch of ingredients come into season together that were just meant for each other. It's during autumn that the first pears start to appear at the markets and arugula is sprouting everywhere in my garden. The sweetness of pear offsets the peppery bite of arugula and, when combined with the crunch of almonds and a punchy chive dressing, you get one of my favorite salads. When I can find them, I use red blush pears for their color pop, but any lovely ripe pear will do.

2 large handfuls of arugula leaves, washed + spun dry

Large handful of baby romaine or crisp iceberg lettuce leaves, washed + spun dry

1 ripe pear

Juice of ½ lemon

¼ cup (40 g) sliced almonds, lightly toasted

chive dressing

3 tablespoons apple cider vinegar

1 teaspoon Dijon mustard

1 teaspoon honey

¼ cup (60 ml) extra-virgin olive oil

1 tablespoon finely chopped chives

+ Place arugula and lettuce in a large bowl. Cut pear into quarters, remove core, and slice thinly. Place in a bowl of cold water with a squeeze of lemon juice to keep it from browning.

+ To make chive dressing, whisk cider vinegar, mustard, and honey together. Whisk continuously as you slowly drizzle in the olive oil to form a lovely emulsified dressing. Stir in chives and season to taste with sea salt and freshly ground black pepper.

+ When ready to serve, drain water from pears and toss through the salad leaves with the toasted almonds and enough dressing to coat. Serve immediately.

SWEET TOOTH

When I was little I always loved helping Mum bake. It's those memories that I still cherish today—the licking of the beaters, the smoothing of the batter in the cake pan and, of course, the eating of the final product (in my mind, it was always banana cake). To me, these moments are a beautiful part of growing up and something that I strive to pass on to my own two children. I know many of you out there today are very concerned about the amount of sugar we eat. I am too, but I don't believe we need to give up sweetness altogether. If we can get all the processed foods out of our lives (or make a good start), get back to eating real food, then I see no harm in having a little sweetness in our lives from time to time. I would much rather watch my children eat a slice of freshly baked cake or a cookie that's been made with whole-grain flours, natural sugars, and plenty of love, than see them eating from a package.

QUINOA + LEMON ANZAC COOKIES MAKES 30

These first appeared on my blog not long after we'd crossed the ditch to live in Perth, Western Australia, and I was missing my grandparents terribly. We've since lost my granddad, but he fills my thoughts every time I make these annual treats. I like my Anzacs crisp on the outside but chewy in the center; if, however, you are one of those crispy-cookie lovers, cook them for 3–4 minutes longer.

1 cup (100 g) quinoa flakes
½ cup (70 g) fine brown rice flour
⅓ cup (40 g) quinoa flour
1 cup (200 g) unrefined raw sugar
¾ cup (75 g) dried coconut
Finely grated zest of 1 lemon
9 tablespoons (125 g) butter
1 tablespoon golden syrup or honey
1 teaspoon baking soda
2 tablespoons boiling water

+ Preheat oven to 335°F (170°C). Grease and line two baking sheets with parchment paper. Place quinoa flakes, brown rice flour, quinoa flour, sugar, coconut, and lemon zest in a bowl. Melt butter and golden syrup together in a small pan over medium heat. Mix baking soda with 2 tablespoons boiling water and add to the dry ingredients along with the melted butter mixture. Mix well with a wooden spoon or clean hands.

+ Roll tablespoons of mixture into balls, squeezing the mixture together if it seems crumbly. Slightly flatten and place about 1-inch apart on baking sheets.

+ Bake for 15–20 minutes until the cookies have risen, then fallen, and become dark golden brown in color. Remove from the oven and set aside for 5 minutes before transferring to a wire rack to cool completely. Store airtight for up to 4–5 days.

SALTED CARAMEL POPCORN SERVES 2–4 . . . OR PERHAPS JUST ONE!

This is the perfect example of not having to compromise on flavor just because you choose to eat healthily. Brown rice syrup provides a mellow sticky sweetness, alongside the buttery coconut oil and a good dash of sea salt for that classic sweet and salty combination. If you can't track down brown rice syrup, use honey. I've given the method for popping corn on the stovetop here, but more often than not I use my little air popcorn popper and then fold in the caramel.

2 tablespoons virgin
coconut oil
½ cup (90 g) popping corn
¼ cup (60 ml) brown rice
syrup
¼ teaspoon fine sea salt

+ Heat 1 tablespoon of the oil in a large heavy-bottomed pan over medium-high heat. Add a few popcorn kernels to the pan, cover, and wait. When they start to pop, add the rest of the kernels, give it all a good shake to evenly coat the kernels in oil, cover, and remove from the heat. Wait for 30 seconds. Give it all another good shake and then return to the heat, with the lid slightly ajar to let steam out. You should start to hear popping after 30–45 seconds. Every now and then give it all a good shake around with the lid on, still allowing a little gap for steam to escape. Once you hear the popping subside (approx. 1–1½ minutes), remove from the heat and transfer to a large bowl.

+ To make the salted caramel, combine brown rice syrup, remaining 1 tablespoon coconut oil, and salt in a small heavy-bottomed saucepan. Bring to a boil over medium heat, whisking constantly. Boil for 30–45 seconds, whisking constantly until mixture thickens and color deepens ever-so-slightly (you are not looking for a dark caramel here and may not even notice the color change). Immediately pour over the popped corn and stir well to coat as best as you can. Set aside for a few minutes to set slightly before digging in. This is not a hard-set caramel, and it's totally fine for it to remain slightly sticky. The popcorn can be stored in an airtight container for 1–2 days, although ours never lasts longer than 30 minutes!

CARROT, APPLE + GINGER MUFFINS MAKES 10

Having worked in cafés for a good portion of my adult life, I can't even begin to imagine how many thousands of muffins I've baked. So perfecting a gluten-free muffin was first on my to-do list when we became aware of our intolerances. On my muffin-recipe checklist was: fast to make, uses readily available ingredients, sweetened with natural alternatives, and tastes as good as any traditional muffin, if not better!

¾ cup (105 g) fine brown rice flour

½ cup (55 g) ground almonds

½ cup (80 g) potato flour

2 teaspoons gluten-free baking powder

¼ teaspoon baking soda

½ teaspoon fine sea salt

1 teaspoon ground cinnamon

1 teaspoon ground ginger

½ cup (125 ml) olive oil

¼ cup (60 ml) honey

1 teaspoon vanilla extract

2 large free-range eggs

2 teaspoons finely grated fresh ginger, optional

1 large carrot, grated

1 apple, skin on and grated

½ cup (80 g) pitted dried dates, finely chopped

Sliced almonds

+ Preheat oven to 350°F (180°C). Grease a 10-hole ⅓ cup (80 ml) muffin tin or line with paper liners. Sift dry ingredients into a bowl then use a whisk to mix together thoroughly. In another bowl combine oil, honey, vanilla, eggs, and grated ginger and pour into dry ingredients. Add carrot, apple, and dates. Stir until just combined.

+ Spoon evenly into tin, sprinkle tops with sliced almonds, and bake for 20–25 minutes or until a skewer inserted into the center of a muffin comes out clean. Set aside for 5 minutes before transferring muffins to a wire rack to cool.

+ These are best eaten on the day of baking, but they will store 1–2 days in an airtight container.

PEACH, ROSEMARY + YOGURT CAKE SERVES 10–12

This is my foolproof simple cake recipe. Its light fluffy texture is perfect for topping with whatever seasonal fruit is lying around. Here I've used tiny golden peaches (my favorites) and a little finely chopped rosemary. But I've also made this with New Zealand black boy peaches from my mum's tree and mangoes fresh from our backyard tree. If you can only get large golden peaches, simply cut them into 4–6 thick wedges. If you prefer to not make the caramel, simply sprinkle 2 tablespoons of unrefined raw or muscovado sugar over the base of the pan instead— just note that it will look a touch different, but still taste fabulous. If using black boy peaches, plums, or mango slices, I would go this route and use unrefined raw sugar.

And, if you don't want to do the whole upside-down cake thing, just chuck a handful of sliced fruit on top of the batter before it goes in the oven. I've used a little ground almond in this mix—for a nut-free version, dried coconut works well in its place.

½ cup (100 g) firmly packed blended unrefined raw sugar + 1 cup (200 g), extra

¼ cup (60 ml) water

1 tablespoon finely chopped rosemary

6 small golden peaches, pitted + halved

12¾ tablespoons (180 g) butter, softened

1 teaspoon vanilla extract

4 large free-range eggs, lightly beaten

⅓ cup (35 g) ground almonds or dried coconut

1 cup (140 g) fine brown rice flour

2 teaspoons gluten-free baking powder

Finely grated zest of 1 lemon

⅓ cup (80 ml) natural plain yogurt

+ Preheat oven to 350°F (180°C). Line the base and side of a 9-inch round springform cake pan with parchment paper and grease well. Place ½ cup sugar and ¼ cup (60 ml) water in a small heavy-bottomed saucepan, stir well, and then bring to a boil over high heat without stirring. Simmer for 4 minutes or until a light caramel forms. Remove from the heat and immediately pour over the bottom of the cake pan. Sprinkle with chopped rosemary, then arrange peach halves over the top, cut-side-down.

+ Cream butter, 1 cup sugar, and vanilla with electric beaters or a wooden spoon until light and fluffy. Gradually add beaten egg, a little at a time, mixing well between each addition. Add ground almonds, then sift in brown rice flour and baking powder. Add lemon zest and yogurt and mix until just combined. Spoon batter over the peaches, smoothing top with a spoon.

+ Bake for 55–60 minutes or until a skewer comes out clean when inserted into the center. Remove from the oven and cool for 5–10 minutes before inverting onto a plate to cool further. Serve slightly warm or at room temperature with a good dollop of natural plain yogurt or softly whipped cream.

CHOCOLATE DATE BLISS BALLS MAKES 14–16

I can't remember a time when there wasn't a batch of these in the fridge. They kept me sane in the early days when we changed our diets and it all seemed too hard. If you live in a place where beautiful plump Medjool dates are not priced like gold, use them in place of the dried. Also keep your eyes open for natural raisins or sultanas at your local health food store—many others are coated in glycerol and hydrogenated oils to keep them from sticking during processing. Hazelnuts make a nice change to the almonds in this recipe and I also make a version using sunflower seeds in place of the nuts if the kids want to take them to school.

1 cup (160 g) pitted dried
  dates
1 cup (200 g) natural
  raisins or sultanas
½ cup (75 g) whole raw
  almonds or sunflower
  seeds
1 tablespoon virgin
  coconut oil
1 teaspoon vanilla extract
¼ cup (15 g) cocoa powder
¼ teaspoon fine sea salt
Shredded coconut,
  to sprinkle

+ Place all ingredients except shredded coconut in a food processor and blend on high for 2–3 minutes until finely ground and starting to clump together in a firm paste. You may need to stop the machine a few times and scrape down the side of the bowl or move things around to assist with blending. Take tablespoons of mixture and roll into balls, roll in shredded coconut, and chill in the fridge for at least 3–4 hours. Will keep, airtight, in the fridge for well over a week.

CHEWY CRANBERRY, MILLET + PISTACHIO BARS MAKES 14

After falling in love with tahini, orange + coconut toasted muesli (page 36), I wanted to come up with something that highlighted those same beautiful tahini flavors. You can find puffed millet in the gluten-free section of bigger supermarkets these days. Failing that, head to a local health food store. If cranberries and pistachio nuts aren't your thing, play around with your favorite nuts and dried fruit. Chopped almonds and dried apricots work well, as do chopped hazelnuts and dried figs. Just cut up the fruit into bite-sized pieces first.

2½ cups (40 g) puffed millet
½ cup (55 g) dried cranberries
¼ cup (30 g) chopped pistachio nuts
½ cup (125 ml) brown rice syrup or ⅓ cup (80 ml) honey
½ cup (125 ml) tahini
3 tablespoons virgin coconut oil
1 teaspoon vanilla extract

+ Grease a 7 x 11-inch baking pan and line with parchment paper (this is a no-bake slice, so don't worry too much about the size and use whatever pan you have, or even a flat plate).

+ Place millet, cranberries, and pistachio nuts in a bowl and give it a good mix. Combine brown rice syrup, tahini, coconut oil, and a good pinch of salt in a small saucepan and bring to a boil over medium heat. The second it starts to bubble around the edges, start stirring to prevent sticking. Simmer for 45 seconds, remove from the heat, and add vanilla. Give it a quick stir before quickly pouring over the millet mixture.

+ Mix well and then transfer to the pan, pressing down evenly with the back of an oiled spoon to compact. Set aside on the counter until cool and then chill in the fridge for 1–2 hours until set. Slice into 14 pieces with a lightly oiled knife. Will store, airtight, in the fridge for up to 1 week (good luck with keeping them around that long!).

RASPBERRY, DARK CHOCOLATE + PISTACHIO BROWNIES MAKES 12

This is intense chocolate brownie at its best. I love the raspberry and pistachios, but there are a million different ways you could take this recipe . . . omit the berries and pistachios, add a touch of cayenne pepper and fold in some lightly toasted chopped almonds. Or keep it humble by just adding the roughly chopped chocolate. Do you want to know the coolest thing about this recipe? I mix the whole lot in the pan I've used to melt the chocolate and oil—this is the fastest cleanup ever.

¾ cup (185 ml) olive oil (use a mild-tasting one here)

7 ounces (200 g) dark chocolate, chopped + ⅓ cup (50 g) chopped, extra

1 cup (200 g) unrefined raw sugar

¼ teaspoon fine sea salt

1 teaspoon vanilla extract

3 large free-range eggs

1 cup (110 g) ground almonds

⅔ cup (90 g) fine brown rice flour

⅓ cup (25 g) cocoa powder

½ teaspoon gluten-free baking powder

1 cup (125 g) raspberries, fresh or frozen

⅓ cup (45 g) pistachio nuts, roughly chopped

+ Preheat oven to 350°F (180°C). Grease and line a 7 x 11-inch baking pan and line with parchment paper, extending up and over the side by 1 inch.

+ Place oil, 7 ounces (200 g) chocolate, sugar, and salt in a saucepan and heat gently, stirring continuously until smooth and melted (it is okay to have some undissolved sugar grains). Remove from heat, add vanilla, and set aside for 5 minutes to cool slightly. Whisk eggs into mixture one at a time, beating well after each addition. Add ground almonds and sift in brown rice flour, cocoa, and baking powder. Mix to combine, then stir in half of the raspberries (if using frozen, don't defrost first), half the extra chocolate, and half the pistachio nuts.

+ Transfer to baking pan, smoothing top with the back of a spoon. Scatter with remaining raspberries, chocolate, and pistachios, pressing the berries into the mixture gently. Bake for 50–55 minutes or until a skewer inserted into the center comes out mostly clean with just a few damp crumbs clinging to it. Remove from the oven and cool in the pan before slicing. Will keep, airtight, at room temperature for 2–3 days or store in the fridge for up to 1 week if you prefer a fudgier brownie (as I do).

GINGER WHOOPIE PIES MAKES 12

When I first moved away from home and started fending for myself in this big, crazy world, I went to the supermarket and bought a whole package of ginger whoopie pies (though we called them kisses) to eat by myself (instead of sharing with four siblings). Naturally, they were one of the first things I converted to gluten-free for this book.

8¾ tablespoons (125 g) butter, softened

¼ cup (50 g) muscovado or soft brown sugar

¼ cup (50 g) firmly packed blended unrefined raw sugar

2 teaspoons molasses or golden syrup

1 teaspoon vanilla extract

2 large free-range eggs

½ cup (60 g) fine quinoa flour

⅓ cup (55 g) potato flour

3 teaspoons ground ginger

½ teaspoon ground cinnamon

½ teaspoon gluten-free baking powder

½ teaspoon baking soda

1 tablespoon boiling water

vanilla buttercream

4¼ tablespoons (60 g) butter, softened

1 cup (125 g) powdered sugar, sifted

1 teaspoon vanilla extract

1 tablespoon boiling water

+ Preheat oven to 335°F (170°C). Grease two 12-hole, 1½ tablespoon (30 ml) capacity, round-based whoopie pie pans. Beat butter, sugars, molasses, and vanilla with electric beaters until light and fluffy (muscovado sugar tends to clump, so do your best to break it up). Add eggs one at a time, beating well after each addition (the mixture will look curdled because the ratio of eggs to butter is high—once the flour is added it will sort itself out). Sift in the flours, spices, and baking powder and fold through until nearly combined. Mix baking soda with 1 tablespoon boiling water and add to the batter, folding in gently until just combined.

+ Spoon into the 24 pan wells (it won't look like much mixture in each pan and don't be tempted to smooth out the tops). Bake for 8–10 minutes or until golden and cooked through when a skewer inserted into the center comes out clean. Remove from the oven and cool for 5 minutes before inverting onto a wire rack to cool completely.

+ To make vanilla buttercream, beat butter, powdered sugar, and vanilla with electric beaters or wooden spoon until light and fluffy, scraping down the side of the bowl with a spatula a few times. Add 1 teaspoon boiling water and beat until mixture loosens and softens.

+ Turn whoopie pie halves the right way up and neaten uneven tops with a sharp serrated knife. Pipe a little bit of frosting onto half the whoopie pies, and sandwich together with the others. Best eaten immediately, but can be stored, airtight, overnight.

LEMON, HONEY + THYME CURD SHORTBREADS MAKES 24

I once worked at a top-end catering company in Sydney where it was my job to make all the desserts and do all the baking. I had just left school, and everything about the place filled me with much excitement. It was the first kitchen I worked in that had separate sections, and being in charge of all things sweet meant that I could avoid working in the area I dreaded most (you got it: the meat section). It also meant that I fine-tuned my baking skills by pumping out tarts, pies, cakes, and cookies by the hundred every day.

These buttery almond shortbreads filled with honey-sweetened lemon curd are my version of a petit four I used to make by the trayful all those years ago. I like to use a floral but not too strongly flavored honey, such as wildflower or clover. You can prepare the shortbreads in advance and fill them before serving, which is always a bonus, I think.

lemon, honey + thyme curd
2 large free-range eggs,
　lightly beaten
⅓ cup (80 ml) honey
Finely grated zest of
　1 large lemon
½ cup (125 ml) freshly
　squeezed lemon juice
3½ tablespoons (50 g)
　butter, diced
3 tablespoons finely
　chopped fresh thyme

almond shortbreads
1 cup (140 g) fine brown
　rice flour
½ cup (50 g) tapioca flour
1 cup (110 g) ground
　almonds
½ cup (100 g) firmly
　packed blended
　unrefined raw sugar
14 tablespoons (200 g)
　butter, slightly softened
Blended unrefined raw
　sugar or powdered
　sugar to dust, optional

+ To make curd, whisk eggs and honey together, add lemon zest and juice and whisk again. Place butter and thyme in a small saucepan over medium heat and heat until butter has just melted but is not overly hot. Whisk in egg mixture and cook over low heat for 6–8 minutes, stirring constantly with a wooden spoon until mixture thickens enough to coat the back of the spoon. Don't let the mixture ever come near boiling point or you'll end up with scrambled eggs.

+ Alternatively, if that chef-style shortcut scares you, put all the curd ingredients in a heatproof bowl set over a saucepan of boiling water and cook, stirring occasionally, for 20 minutes or until lovely and thick. Strain through a fine sieve, discarding zest and thyme. Transfer to a clean jar and cool before sealing and chilling in the fridge to firm up further. Use within a week.

+ To make shortbreads, place flours, ground almonds, and sugar in a food processor and pulse to combine. Add butter and pulse a few times until a soft dough forms. Transfer to a lightly rice-floured countertop, shape into a flat disc, wrap and chill in the fridge for 1 hour.

+ Preheat oven to 335°F (170°C). Grease 24 mini-muffin tins. Roll tablespoons of dough into balls and place one in each tin, without flattening. Bake for 12–15 minutes until light golden brown. Remove from the oven and, using the round handle of a wooden spoon or whisk, press down into the center of each shortbread to form a little indent. Set aside to cool in the tins. When cold, remove from tins (use the tip of a sharp knife inserted down one side of the shortbread to gently encourage it up and out of the tin—you may get a few breakages, but I just think of these as "chef testers"). Pipe or spoon a small amount of lemon curd into each one. Dust with raw sugar or powdered sugar to serve. Unfilled shortbreads will store, airtight, for up to 3 days.

BANANA, DATE + OLIVE OIL BREAD MAKES 1 LOAF

This loaf appeared on my blog in the middle of recipe testing for this book, and I quickly realized it had become my favorite way to use up the overripe bananas doing their thing in the fruit bowl. Since the blog posting, a few things have come and gone: I now sweeten with just a touch of maple syrup (or honey) instead of sugar and prefer the lightness of potato starch to the original tapioca. To be honest, any starch works fine so use whichever one you have in the cupboard: tapioca, corn, or potato.

1 cup (160 g) pitted dried dates, finely chopped

1 teaspoon baking soda

2 tablespoons boiling water

1½ cups mashed overripe banana (about 3 large bananas)

½ cup (125 ml) olive oil

2 tablespoons pure maple syrup

2 large free-range eggs, lightly beaten

1 teaspoon vanilla extract

Finely grated zest of 1 lemon

1½ cups (210 g) fine brown rice flour

½ cup (80 g) potato flour

2 teaspoons gluten-free baking powder

Sunflower and pumpkin seeds (pepitas), to sprinkle

+ Preheat oven to 350°F (180°C). Grease and line a loaf pan with parchment paper, extending over the sides by about 1 inch. I use my deep 8 x 4 x 3-inch bread pan, but any loaf pan will do.

+ Stir together chopped dates, baking soda, and 2 tablespoons boiling water in a small bowl. In a large bowl combine mashed banana, olive oil, maple syrup, eggs, vanilla, and lemon zest and whisk until smooth. Sift brown rice flour, potato flour, baking powder, and a good pinch of fine sea salt over the banana mixture, stir until nearly combined, and then add dates and any remaining liquid from them. Stir to form a soft batter.

+ Transfer batter to loaf pan, scatter with a few sunflower and pumpkin seeds, and bake for 1–1¼ hours or until a skewer comes out clean when inserted into the center of the loaf. Remove from oven and set aside for 5–10 minutes before transferring to a wire rack to cool. Best left until completely cold before slicing. Will keep for 3 days if stored airtight or can be frozen in thick slices for 2–3 months.

SPICED PUMPKIN, DATE + QUINOA MUFFINS MAKES 6

It was during my home economics class in high school that I first learned to make muffins properly. All those muffin-making rules still rattle around in my head every time I make a batch, talking me through the process like an obsessive old woman: add wet to dry; don't overmix; scoop the mixture up in one go when transferring it to the tins (this prevents those crazy mountain peaks you can see in wheat-flour muffins). Do you know something? None of these rules, except the first, applies to gluten-free muffins. Mix all you like, they still won't get tough. Didn't get enough mixture on that spoon to fill up the tin? No worries, just top it up with another spoonful. Gluten-free muffins really are very forgiving.

½ cup (115 g) pumpkin puree (see NOTE)

Finely grated zest of 1 orange

1 large free-range egg

¼ cup (60 ml) olive oil

⅓ cup (80 ml) rice, almond, or coconut milk

½ teaspoon vanilla extract

½ cup (70 g) fine brown rice flour

¼ cup (30 g) fine quinoa flour

1½ teaspoons gluten-free baking powder

½ teaspoon ground cinnamon

½ teaspoon ground ginger

¼ cup (50 g) unrefined raw sugar

¼ cup (25 g) ground almonds

⅓ cup (55 g) pitted dried dates, finely chopped

1 tablespoon quinoa flakes, optional

+ Preheat oven to 350°F (180°C) and grease a 6-hole ⅓ cup (80 ml) muffin tin. Whisk together pumpkin, orange zest, egg, oil, milk, and vanilla extract until smooth. In another larger bowl sift together brown rice flour, quinoa flour, baking powder, cinnamon, and ginger. Add raw sugar, ground almonds, a good pinch of fine sea salt, and dates. Whisk to thoroughly combine, then make a well in the center and pour in the pumpkin mixture. Stir until just combined.

+ Spoon into tin, sprinkle tops with quinoa flakes if using, and bake for 20–25 minutes or until golden and a skewer comes out clean when poked into the center. Cool in the tin for 5 minutes before transferring to a wire rack to cool completely. Best eaten on day of baking but will store, airtight, for up to 2 days.

NOTE: To make pumpkin puree, steam chunks of pumpkin until soft. Mash well or puree and cool before using. Any leftover puree can be frozen in ziplock bags for next time.

CHOCOLATE COCONUT CUPCAKES MAKES 12

These are the cupcakes I bake for the kids to share with the class on their birthdays. Being free from gluten, dairy, egg, and nuts pretty much covers most of the allergies that we come across at school, which means everyone can eat one. They're ridiculously easy to make and taste better than any wheat-based cupcake I remember. I've lost count of how many times I've been asked for this recipe from teachers and mums—and these are people who don't even need to eat allergy-free! For the ganache I use a 50% dark chocolate, as I find anything darker is a bit too rich when mixed with coconut milk.

14-ounce (400 ml) can coconut milk

¾ cup (150 g) unrefined raw sugar

⅓ cup (80 ml) olive oil or virgin coconut oil, melted

2 teaspoons apple cider vinegar

1 teaspoon vanilla extract

½ cup (70 g) fine brown rice flour

⅓ cup (55 g) potato flour

⅓ cup (25 g) cocoa powder

¾ teaspoon baking soda

½ teaspoon gluten-free baking powder

⅓ cup (30 g) dried coconut

¼ teaspoon fine sea salt

chocolate coconut ganache

½ cup (125 ml) coconut milk

6 ounces (180 g) dark chocolate, roughly chopped

Freshly shaved coconut or toasted dried coconut flakes, to serve, optional

+ Preheat oven to 350°F (180°C). Line a 12-hole ⅓ cup (80 ml) muffin tin with paper liners.

+ Whisk together coconut milk, sugar, oil, vinegar, and vanilla until smooth. In another bowl sift brown rice flour, potato flour, cocoa, baking soda, and baking powder. Add dried coconut and salt and whisk to combine all the dry ingredients. Make a well in the center and pour in coconut milk mixture, whisking until a smooth-ish batter forms. Spoon into tin and bake for 18–20 minutes or until a skewer comes out clean when inserted into the center. Cool 5 minutes in the tin, then transfer to a wire rack to cool completely. Frost when cool.

+ To make the chocolate coconut ganache, bring the coconut milk to a boil in a small saucepan. Remove from heat and add chocolate. Set aside for 1 minute, then stir until melted and smooth. Spoon on top of the cooled cupcakes and sprinkle with fresh or toasted coconut.

CHOUX PUFFS WITH LABNEH + STRAWBERRY JAM

MAKES APPROX. 35 BITE-SIZED PUFFS

Growing up, I loved nothing more than a good cream bun or chocolate éclair. Anything that had cream on it, I was there with my hand outstretched, waiting impatiently for more. Sadly, now I only allow myself the pleasure of real cream on special occasions, but labneh is a very good stand-in. Here I've used it to offset the sweetness of the gorgeous homemade jam.

7 tablespoons (100 g) butter, cubed

Pinch each of fine sea salt and unrefined raw sugar

½ cup (70 g) fine brown rice flour

¼ cup (35 g) buckwheat flour

¼ cup (25 g) gluten-free organic cornstarch

4 large free-range eggs, lightly beaten

1 cup labneh (page 222)

Strawberry thyme jam, to serve (page 228)

+ Preheat oven to 400°F (200°C) and line two baking sheets with parchment paper.

+ Place butter, salt, sugar, and 1 cup (250 ml) water in a small heavy-bottomed pan over medium heat and bring to a boil, stirring to fully melt the butter. Sift flours and cornstarch into a small bowl and then whisk to fully combine. As soon as the water bubbles and comes to a rolling boil, add the combined flours all at once and beat continuously with a wooden spoon as it thickens. Continue beating until the dough is smooth and comes away from the side of the pan cleanly. It will seem a little greasy and the buckwheat flour will cause it to look a tad gray—this is okay.

+ Transfer dough to a bowl, flatten it out to help it cool faster, and set aside for 5 minutes. Start adding the beaten eggs, a little bit at a time, beating well after each addition with a handheld beater or wooden spoon until the mixture just falls from the spoon but still holds its shape. You may not need to add the very last little bit of egg, so save to use as the egg wash.

+ Transfer mixture to a piping bag fitted with a ½-inch plain nozzle and pipe small rounds of mixture (approx. 2–3 teaspoons each) onto trays, leaving at least 1 inch of room for spreading. If you don't have a piping bag, simply drop small spoonfuls of dough onto the trays. Brush tops with a little leftover egg and bake for 25–30 minutes or until puffed and golden.

+ Turn off the oven and remove choux buns. Pierce a small hole in the underside of each puff with a small knife, letting the steam escape. Put the puffs back into the cooling oven and leave for another 15 minutes to dry out further. Remove from the oven and transfer to a wire rack to cool completely.

+ Serve choux puffs torn in half, spread with labneh and strawberry jam. Best served on the day of baking; however, unfilled choux puffs will store, airtight, for 1–2 days.

DARK CHOCOLATE, BUCKWHEAT + PEAR LOAF MAKES 1 LOAF

I first made this loaf a few years back, using the flesh of the supersoft, astringent Hachiya persimmon. It was amazing, but knowing that most of the year people are hard-pressed to get their hands on these, I've played around with pureed pear instead. This isn't the sort of loaf you might be used to—it's almost pudding-like in its texture. It's lovely eaten warm from the oven with the chocolate still melted in little puddles, but also good served cold, thickly sliced, with a cup of fruity herb tea.

½ cup (125 ml) coconut milk

¾ teaspoon lemon juice or apple cider vinegar

3 large free-range eggs, lightly beaten

⅓ cup (80 ml) olive oil

½ teaspoon vanilla extract

1½ cups (375 g) cooked pureed pear (see NOTE)

½ cup (65 g) roughly chopped dark chocolate

⅓ cup (65 g) unrefined raw sugar

⅓ cup (35 g) ground almonds

⅓ cup (46 g) buckwheat flour

⅓ cup (46 g) fine brown rice flour

1 teaspoon gluten-free baking powder

½ teaspoon baking soda

¼ teaspoon fine sea salt

+ Preheat oven to 190°C (375°F). Grease a loaf pan and line with a strip of parchment paper that covers the bottom and comes up and over the sides by about 1 inch. I use my deep 8 x 4 x 3-inch bread pan, but any loaf pan will do.

+ Combine coconut milk and lemon juice or vinegar in a bowl and set aside for 5 minutes. Add eggs, olive oil, vanilla extract, and pear puree and whisk until smooth.

+ Tip chocolate, sugar, and ground almonds into a large bowl. Sift in flours, baking powder, baking soda, and salt and whisk to combine. Pour in the egg mixture and stir until just combined. Pour into the pan and bake for 55–60 minutes or until a skewer comes out clean when inserted into the center. If you are having trouble finding a piece of loaf to test that doesn't just leave your skewer covered in melted chocolate, use your finger to test instead. Press gently in the center of the loaf and, if it's done, it will bounce back. Remove from oven and cool in the pan for 5 minutes before transferring to a wire rack to cool completely. Will keep, airtight, for up to 3 days or for longer in the fridge.

NOTE: To make pear puree, put 3 large peeled, cored, and finely sliced pears in a saucepan with a couple of tablespoons of water. Cover with a lid and bring to a boil; reduce the heat and simmer for 8–10 minutes or until soft. Remove from the heat and puree until smooth. You need 1½ cups for this recipe—any extra is delicious stirred into plain yogurt, or make a double batch and freeze some for next time. You could also use apple puree.

DARK CHOCOLATE COCONUT BITES MAKES APPROX. 28

I've always loved a certain kind of dark chocolate bar with a chewy coconut filling—no names necessary here, I'm sure! There was a stage in my life when I found it near impossible to walk past the sweets aisle at the supermarket without grabbing one, or two. As soon as I started cooking with coconut oil and realized its amazing setting properties, I got onto developing my own version. These keep in the fridge for ages, so are a lovely treat to have tucked away. If brown rice syrup isn't easily available where you live, use ¼ cup (60 ml) pure maple syrup or honey instead (the center will be slightly darker, but delicious nonetheless).

3 cups (270 g) shredded or dried coconut

⅓ cup (80 ml) brown rice syrup

¼ cup (60 ml) virgin coconut oil

8½ ounces (250 g) dark chocolate, roughly chopped

+ Place coconut, brown rice syrup, coconut oil, and a good pinch of fine sea salt in a food processor and blend on high for 1–2 minutes, stopping to scrape down the side of the bowl once or twice. You want the mixture to be finely ground and everything evenly distributed. Press mixture evenly into two ice-cube trays, making sure you compact the mixture down as much as possible, leaving no big gaps. Chill in the fridge for 1 hour or until set.

+ Twist trays to release coconut bites. Melt chopped chocolate in a clean dry heatproof bowl set over a saucepan of boiling water (make sure the bottom is not touching the water) and stir with a metal spoon until just liquid. Set aside for 5 minutes to cool slightly. Dip each coconut bite into the chocolate, coating evenly on all sides. Use two forks to transfer bites to a parchment-paper lined tray, allowing as much excess chocolate as possible to drip from the bite before setting it down. Let the chocolate set. (If it's a really hot day, chill them in the fridge for 10 minutes instead.) Store in an airtight container in the fridge and then allow them to come to room temperature for 10 minutes before eating—although, really, who has that kind of restraint?

BIG PLATES

Dinner always started with a moment of silence as my parents meditated and we kids tried hard not to make faces at each other. Much of what we ate came straight from the garden at the bottom of the very steep hill below our house. I remember lots of brown rice, loads of vegetables, and always a huge bowlful of salad. Unlike my mother's gorgeous (but labor-intensive) meals, dinner in my house today is usually a quick and easy affair. As any busy parent knows, there's not a lot of time left to create elaborate meals, unless you're prepared to spend much of the day cooking, as my mum did. Most children don't wait patiently for dinner and require feeding as early as possible (to avoid all-out war at 6 p.m.) so during the week I turn to a trusted selection of dishes that can be made in advance and put together quickly. I've also included favorite recipes here, some of which do require advance planning but give impressive results, and some that I've learned during the years of watching over the shoulder of my mother-in-law in her Vietnamese kitchen. Being short on time is never an excuse to order takeout. I don't feel any shame in serving crispy fried eggs on rice with furikake (page 232) and salad on busy nights, and I don't think you should either.

BÁNH XÈO (CRISPY PANCAKES)
SERVES 4–5 PEOPLE WITH 2–3 PANCAKES PER PERSON

I first fell in love with these addictive Vietnamese crispy rice flour pancakes when Si and I traveled through Southeast Asia in our early twenties. My mother-in-law is famed for her bánh xèo; when the kids were little, I used to talk about Bà Noˆi's bánh xèo so much that they once made them for me, out of playdough. Bánh xèo are best eaten screaming hot, straight from the pan, so you can fry and serve one at a time, or get fancy and cook with two or three pans as my mother-in-law does.

pancake batter

2 cups (250 g) fine white rice flour
1 tablespoon potato starch or organic gluten-free cornstarch
½ teaspoon unrefined raw sugar
1 teaspoon fine sea salt
1 teaspoon ground turmeric
1 cup (250 ml) coconut milk
2 cups (500 ml) cold water
2 tablespoons chopped chives or the green part of 1 spring onion
Olive oil

pancake filling

½ cup (100 g) whole dried mung beans
4 cups (1 liter) cold water
12-ounce (350 g) package firm tofu, rinsed + patted dry with paper towels
1 large onion, finely sliced
2 big handfuls (approx. 300–400 g) mung bean sprouts

dipping sauce

¼ cup (50 g) unrefined raw sugar
1 teaspoon fine sea salt
¼ cup (60 ml) boiling water
¼ cup (60 ml) gluten-free soy sauce
¼ cup (60 ml) lemon juice

to serve

Iceberg lettuce leaves
Mint leaves
2–3 bird's eye chilies, deseeded + finely chopped
2 garlic cloves, finely chopped

+ To make batter, place rice flour, potato starch, sugar, salt, and turmeric in a large bowl. Whisk in coconut milk and 2 cups (500 ml) cold water to form a smooth batter with the consistency of pouring cream. Stir in chives, cover, and set aside at room temperature for 30–60 minutes or chill overnight (you might need to add a little water the next day to thin it to pouring consistency).

+ To make filling, put mung beans in a saucepan, cover with 4 cups (1 liter) cold water, bring to a boil, then turn down to a simmer and cook for 25 minutes or until tender but not falling apart. Refresh under cold water to stop them from cooking further. Cut tofu into ½-inch slices and, working in batches, cook in a touch of oil in a hot frying pan over medium heat until golden on both sides. Remove from the pan and slice each piece into long strips about ¼-inch wide.

+ To make dipping sauce, mix sugar, salt, and boiling water in a small bowl until dissolved. Add soy sauce and lemon juice and mix well. This can be stored in a glass jar in the fridge for up to 1 week.

+ When ready to eat, set the table with a large platter of lettuce and mint leaves and bowls of dipping sauce, adding a little of the chilis and garlic to each bowl, if you like. Have your filling ingredients and batter right next to the stove. Heat an 8-inch frying pan or wok over high heat, add 1 tablespoon of olive oil and a few slices of onion. Stir-fry for 30–60 seconds until lightly browned, add 5–6

slices of tofu, and stir to heat through briefly. Pour about ½ cup (100 ml) batter into the pan, swirling so it covers the base and slightly up the sides of the pan in a thin crepe-like film. Scatter with 1 tablespoon mung beans and arrange a handful of mung bean sprouts down one side of the pancake. Cover with a lid, reduce heat slightly and cook for 3–5 minutes until the base is golden and crispy. Fold pancake in half to enclose the filling and serve immediately. Make the rest in the same way, giving the batter a good stir between pancakes as the flour has a tendency to settle to the bottom of the bowl.

+ To eat, take a piece of lettuce in your hand, top with a few mint leaves, tear off a little bit of pancake, making sure you get some mung bean sprouts as well, and roll this up in the lettuce and mint. Dip into the sauce and dig in.

SPICE-ROASTED VEGETABLES WITH CHICKPEAS, MILLET + CHERMOULA

SERVES 4–6

When we first changed our diets, I'd sometimes open the fridge, look around for something I could eat with a baby and toddler hanging off my hip and then close it again a few seconds later, empty-handed and hungry. I lived off roasted root vegetables and cooked quinoa or millet, as everything else just seemed too involved for my tired brain to deal with. Now that things aren't so strict and I have more time, I've added a few of my favorite things to those sanity-saving roasted root vegetables—chickpeas, spices, and a punchy cilantro-based sauce—to create a lovely late winter/early spring dish with a bit of attitude.

¾ cup (135 g) dried chickpeas, soaked overnight in cold water, or 14-ounce (400 g) can cooked chickpeas, rinsed well

3 tablespoons olive oil

2 tablespoons finely chopped cilantro stems

2 garlic cloves, finely chopped

1 teaspoon coriander seeds, roughly ground

3 teaspoons cumin seeds

1 teaspoon paprika

½ teaspoon ground cinnamon

1 teaspoon honey

1 teaspoon sea salt

½ teaspoon freshly ground black pepper

Finely grated zest of 1 lemon

1 bunch 6–9 baby beets (approx. 11 ounces), stalks trimmed to about 1 inch

1 bunch (approx. 12) baby carrots, stalks trimmed to about 1 inch

2 small parsnips, cut into quarters lengthwise

Mint leaves, to serve

millet

1 tablespoon olive oil

1 cup (210 g) hulled millet

2 cups (500 ml) water

chermoula

1 cup chopped cilantro leaves and stems

¼ cup (60 ml) extra-virgin olive oil

Juice of ½ lemon

1 garlic clove, roughly chopped

½ teaspoon ground coriander

½ teaspoon ground cumin

+ Drain and rinse chickpeas. Place in a saucepan, cover with plenty of cold water, and bring to a boil, skimming off any foam that rises to the surface. Reduce to a simmer and cook for 25–35 minutes or until tender but not falling apart. Drain well.

+ Preheat oven to 350°F (180°C). Place olive oil, cilantro stems, garlic, spices, honey, salt, pepper and lemon zest in a large bowl and mix well. If your baby beets are wider than an inch, cut them in half so that they're the same thickness as the carrots and parsnips for even cooking. Add chickpeas, beets, carrots, and parsnips to bowl and mix well to coat. Transfer to a baking dish and spread out in a single layer. Roast for 45–50 minutes, stirring at least once, until golden and tender. (If you are overly concerned with the color bleeding from the beets, keep them at one end of the tray.)

+ Meanwhile, to cook the millet, heat oil in a saucepan, add millet, and stir constantly for 3–4 minutes until toasty smelling. Carefully add 2 cups (500 ml) water (take care as it will splutter a bit) and a pinch of salt, cover the pan, and bring to a boil. Reduce heat and simmer for 20 minutes or until all the water has been absorbed and the millet is tender. Remove from the heat, keep the lid on, and let sit and steam for 5 minutes before fluffing up with a fork.

+ To make chermoula, put all ingredients into a blender or food processor and blend on high until cilantro is finely chopped and a rough sauce forms. Season to taste with sea salt.

+ Serve millet topped with roasted vegetables and chickpeas, making sure you scrape up all those lovely spices from the tray. Drizzle with a little chermoula and scatter with mint leaves.

TOFU STIR-FRY WITH PICKLED CARROT, CASHEW + CHILI SERVES 4

There are two things I've learned from marrying into a Vietnamese family: forget about marinating raw tofu to add flavor (you need to fry the tofu until crisp before you flavor with sauces); and always add something acidic to a tofu stir-fry. A squeeze of lime works well, or here I've added a little pickled carrot to give a lovely sour tang. You'll need to start this recipe at least a couple of hours in advance to give the carrot time to pickle. When you use the carrot, don't throw away the pickling liquid, but finely slice another large carrot and mix it into the jar for next time. It will keep in a covered container or glass jar in the fridge for up to 1 week. To make this an everyday dish, I always keep whole Kaffir lime leaves, grated ginger, and whole red chilies in ziplock bags in my freezer. And don't have snow peas? Any Asian greens will work. Have all the ingredients chopped and ready before you start stir-frying, including cooked jasmine rice to serve.

2–3 tablespoons olive oil

12-ounce (350 g) package extra firm tofu, rinsed, drained + patted dry with a clean tea towel then cut into 1-inch dice

2 garlic cloves, finely chopped

1 tablespoon finely grated ginger

1 long red chili (cayenne or Thai), finely sliced

3 whole Kaffir lime leaves

1 tomato, finely diced

3 spring onions, cut into 2-inch lengths

Large handful of snow peas, trimmed + strings removed

¼ cup (60 ml) gluten-free soy sauce

1 tablespoon unrefined raw sugar

1 cup (125 g) lightly toasted cashews

Handful of Thai basil leaves, optional

Cooked jasmine rice, to serve

pickled carrot

¼ cup (50 g) unrefined raw sugar

¼ teaspoon fine sea salt

¼ cup (60 ml) boiling water

¼ cup (60 ml) rice vinegar

1 large carrot, cut into long fine strips (use a mandoline, if you have one)

+ To pickle the carrot, stir together sugar, salt, and boiling water in a glass or ceramic bowl until dissolved. Add rice vinegar and set aside until cool. Pack carrot into a glass jar or container, pour in cooled vinegar mixture, cover, and place in the fridge for at least 2 hours or overnight.

+ Heat a large frying pan or wok over high heat, add 1–2 tablespoons olive oil and cook tofu for 8–10 minutes, turning to brown evenly on all sides. Transfer tofu to a plate and return pan to the heat. Add another tablespoon of oil if needed and quickly stir-fry garlic, ginger, and chili for 30 seconds until fragrant. Add lime leaves and tomato and cook for another 30–45 seconds until tomato is tender. Add the white ends of the spring onion and snow peas and return tofu to the pan. Stir-fry for 1 minute before adding the green ends of the spring onions, soy sauce, sugar, and drained pickled carrot. Cook for 1–2 minutes or until the sauce has reduced and vegetables are just tender. Remove from the heat, and toss through toasted cashews and Thai basil leaves, if using. Season with black pepper and serve with cooked jasmine rice.

PEANUT BROWN RICE PATTIES SERVES 4

My mother would make these if meat-eating friends were coming for dinner. They were always served alongside buttery mashed potatoes, boiled peas, and carrots—a vegetarian's version of "meat and potatoes." I use quinoa flakes, but if you tolerate whole-grain rolled oats, that's what Mum always uses. To keep these vegan, use olive oil to panfry, but I usually cook these in ghee. The mixture will keep in the fridge for three days, making this easy to prepare in advance.

1 cup (150 g) raw peanuts
1 cup (140 g) cooked brown rice
1 cup (100 g) quinoa flakes or whole-grain rolled oats
Small handful of flat-leaf parsley leaves, roughly chopped
1 tablespoon olive oil
½ large onion, finely diced
1 garlic clove, finely chopped
1 teaspoon dried oregano
1 teaspoon finely chopped fresh thyme
2 tablespoons white (shiro) miso paste
½ cup (125 ml) boiling water
Olive oil or ghee
Tomato chutney or sauce, to serve

+ Place peanuts in a blender or food processor and blend until finely ground. Transfer to a large bowl and add rice, quinoa flakes, and flat-leaf parsley.

+ Heat olive oil in a small frying pan over medium heat and cook onion for 3–4 minutes, stirring often until tender. Add garlic, oregano, and thyme and cook for another 1–2 minutes until fragrant. Add to the peanut mixture. Stir miso paste into boiling water to dissolve and then add to the bowl. I usually get my hands in at this stage to thoroughly mix everything together. Season to taste with salt and black pepper.

+ Roll mixture into golf ball–sized portions, flatten to form patties (approx. 12 small patties or 8 larger ones), and set aside while you heat up a large heavy-bottomed frying pan over medium-high heat. Add a few glugs of olive oil or a couple of tablespoons of ghee to your hot pan and panfry patties in batches for 2–3 minutes each side or until golden brown, crisp on the outside and warmed through in the center. Transfer to a paper towel–lined plate to drain while you cook the rest. Serve with tomato chutney.

ROASTED CHERRY TOMATO QUICHE WITH CHICKPEA CRUST SERVES 4–6

This is the easiest piecrust to make, requires no fiddly rolling out, and, unlike many other gluten-free pastries, doesn't disintegrate into crumbs when you bite into it. This is what I make at the peak of summer when our tomato plants are going into overdrive and I'm scrambling to use up hundreds of cherry tomatoes.

chickpea crust

¾ cup (135 g) dried chickpeas, soaked in cold water overnight, or 14-ounce (400 g) can cooked chickpeas, rinsed, or 1½ cups cooked chickpeas

¼ cup (35 g) fine brown rice flour

2 tablespoons tapioca flour or gluten-free organic cornstarch

½ teaspoon gluten-free baking powder

1½ tablespoons olive oil

½ teaspoon fine sea salt

filling

1 pound (500 g) cherry tomatoes, cut in half

2 garlic cloves, finely chopped

1 tablespoon finely chopped thyme

3 tablespoons extra-virgin olive oil

4 large free-range eggs

¾ cup (185 ml) coconut, almond, or rice milk

½ cup firmly packed basil leaves, finely shredded + extra, to serve

2 teaspoons Dijon mustard

2 tablespoons finely chopped chives

2 tablespoons finely chopped flat-leaf parsley

½ teaspoon fine sea salt

¼ teaspoon freshly ground black pepper

+ Drain and rinse chickpeas. Place in a saucepan and cover with plenty of fresh cold water. Bring to a boil, skimming off any foam that rises to the surface. Reduce to a simmer and cook for 25–35 minutes or until tender but not falling apart. Drain well and set aside to cool slightly. Preheat oven to 350°F (180°C). Grease a 12½ x 4¾-inch loose-bottom fluted tart pan or a 9-inch round loose-bottom tart pan.

+ Arrange tomatoes cut-side-up on a baking sheet, scatter with garlic and thyme, drizzle with olive oil, and season well with sea salt and freshly ground black pepper. Roast for 30 minutes or until tender and slightly dried.

+ Meanwhile, to make crust, pulse chickpeas in a food processor until finely ground (a few lumps are okay). Transfer to a bowl and add brown rice flour, tapioca flour, and baking powder. Mix thoroughly with your hands, add oil and salt, and mix to a stiff dough. Press evenly into the tin, lining the base and sides, and using the back of a spoon to firmly press down. Bake for 6–8 minutes to lightly set—don't be tempted to cook the crust for any longer than this or it will start to crack and you'll lose all your filling. Scatter two-thirds of the roasted tomatoes and herbs over the crust.

+ Whisk together eggs, milk, basil, mustard, herbs, and seasoning and pour into the crust. Bake for 45–55 minutes or until golden brown and set. Let sit for 5 minutes before serving. If you are not serving immediately, remove from the pan and transfer to a wire rack to prevent the crust from sweating and becoming soggy. Top with remaining roasted tomatoes and extra basil leaves to serve.

BAKED BUTTERBEANS WITH TOMATO + FETA SERVES 4–6

This is a perfect weekday dinner in that it can be prepared in advance and then just popped into the oven for the final bake. If you own a large ovenproof frying pan (cast iron is perfect), you can make and cook this all in the one pan—always a bonus in my book. If I'm lucky, I have enough tomato + basil sauce in the freezer to last me at least half of the year, but sometimes I use a tin of whole peeled tomatoes instead and add 1 teaspoon unrefined raw sugar to bring out the flavor.

¼ cup (60 ml) extra-virgin olive oil

1 large onion, finely diced

1 celery stalk, finely diced

1 large carrot, finely diced

3 garlic cloves, finely chopped

1 teaspoon dried oregano

1 teaspoon fresh thyme leaves, roughly chopped

1 recipe tomato + basil sauce (page 234) or 14-ounce (400 g) can whole peeled tomatoes

2 tablespoons tomato paste diluted in ¾ cup (185 ml) hot water

3 cups cooked butterbeans or two 14-ounce (400 g) cans butterbeans, rinsed (see NOTE)

¼ cup roughly chopped flat-leaf parsley

3½ ounces (100 g) firm feta cheese, crumbled

+ Preheat oven to 350°F (180°C). Heat olive oil in a large frying pan over medium heat (if you have an ovenproof pan, use it). Add onion, celery, carrot, garlic, oregano, and thyme and cook for 8–10 minutes, stirring often until onion is translucent. Add tomato sauce or canned tomatoes with sugar and tomato paste mixture. Cover and cook for another 10 minutes or until the vegetables are tender.

+ Stir in butterbeans and parsley. Season to taste with sea salt and black pepper and transfer to a large ovenproof dish (no need, if you're using an ovensafe frying pan). Scatter with feta and bake, uncovered, for 30 minutes. Serve with bread or cooked rice and salad.

NOTE: If cooking beans from scratch, soak 1 cup dried beans overnight in plenty of cold water at room temperature. In hot weather put soaking beans in the fridge. The next day, drain off water and refill with plenty of fresh cold water. Bring to a boil, skimming off any foam that rises to the surface, and simmer gently for about 1 hour, or until tender but not falling apart. Top up with extra water if needed. Add a few pinches of sea salt and cook for another 5 minutes before draining well.

CHICKPEA, PUMPKIN + KALE STEW WITH CHIMICHURRI + QUINOA

SERVES 4–6

Pumpkin, loads of spices, tomato, chickpeas, hearty kale, chili, and lime are the basis of this South American–inspired dish. It's perfect for the start of autumn, when fresh pumpkins are coming into season and end of the summer tomatoes are (almost) a dime a dozen. I love the humble pumpkin and think its greatness should be celebrated more often. One large pumpkin is very cheap and will provide enough flesh to make four or five different meals. They're super-easy to grow (just whack a handful of seeds from any pumpkin into well-composted soil and then be amazed as they take over your garden beds and lawn), and your pumpkin harvest can be stored all year without showing any signs of age.

¾ cup (135 g) dried chickpeas, soaked in cold water overnight, or 14-ounce (400 g) can cooked chickpeas, rinsed, or 1½ cups cooked chickpeas

2 tablespoons olive oil

1 red onion, finely diced

4 garlic cloves, finely chopped

1 long red chili (cayenne or Thai), deseeded and finely chopped

1 teaspoon thyme, finely chopped

1 teaspoon dried oregano

1 teaspoon paprika

2 fresh or dried bay leaves

6 ripe tomatoes, cored, peeled + roughly chopped (NOTE on page 234), or 14-ounce (400 g) can whole peeled tomatoes

2 tablespoons tomato paste

1 teaspoon unrefined raw sugar

2½ cups (approx. 400 g) diced pumpkin flesh

1½ cups (375 ml) water

4 large kale leaves, hard stems removed and leaves finely chopped

Juice of ½ lime

Cooked quinoa (page 20) and extra-virgin olive oil, to serve

chimichurri

1 cup firmly packed mint leaves

1 cup firmly packed flat-leaf parsley leaves

2 garlic cloves, roughly chopped

1 long green chili, deseeded + roughly chopped

1 teaspoon cumin seeds, lightly toasted + finely ground

3 tablespoons lime juice

3 tablespoons extra-virgin olive oil

½ teaspoon fine sea salt

+ Drain and rinse chickpeas, put in a saucepan, and cover with cold water. Bring to a boil, skimming any foam that rises to the surface. Reduce to a simmer and cook for 25–35 minutes or until tender but not falling apart. Drain well.

+ Heat oil in a large saucepan over medium heat. Add onion, garlic, chili, thyme, and oregano and cook, stirring, for 5–8 minutes until tender and fragrant. Add paprika and bay leaves and cook for another minute. Stir in chopped tomatoes, tomato paste, and sugar and season with plenty of sea salt and black pepper. Simmer for 5 minutes or until pulpy. Add pumpkin and 1½ cups (375 ml) water, stir well, and return to a boil. Cover partially and simmer gently for 10–15 minutes until pumpkin is tender. Stir in kale and chickpeas, cover again, and cook for 5 minutes until kale is wilted and chickpeas are hot. Stir in lime juice and season to taste with sea salt and freshly ground black pepper. Serve hot over quinoa with a generous drizzle of chimichurri and extra-virgin olive oil.

+ To make the chimichurri, place all ingredients in a food processor and blend for 1–2 minutes, scraping down the bowl a few times until herbs are finely chopped. Alternatively, chop herbs, garlic, and chili as finely as you can with a sharp knife and stir in remaining ingredients, or bash it all together with a mortar and pestle.

TOFU CURRY WITH CHILI + TAMARIND SERVES 3–4

I love curries. For me, this is comfort food at its best. I like to use dried Kashmiri chilies for their intense red color and relatively mild heat factor (but really any long red dried chili will do). Kashmiri chilies are easily found at your local Indian grocery store, as are the fresh curry leaves, tamarind, and asafoetida. Asafoetida, also known as hing, is a pungent yellow powder made from the dried root gum of a plant similar to fennel. The most common powdered form has wheat added to it, probably to prevent clumping, so if you are supersensitive to gluten and can't find the pure resin form, just omit it from the recipe. Fresh curry leaves are always sold in bunches; any leftover leaves can be frozen in ziplock bags and used without defrosting.

11 dried (25 g) Kashmiri chilies (or long red dried chilies)

2 teaspoons cumin seeds, lightly toasted

4 garlic cloves, roughly chopped

1 tablespoon ghee or olive oil

12-ounce (350 g) package firm tofu, rinsed, patted dry + cut into 1-inch cubes

¾ cup (185 ml) water

¼ cup tamarind puree (see NOTE)

2 tablespoons tomato paste

1 stem of fresh curry leaves, stalk discarded

Pinch of asafoetida, optional

1 teaspoon unrefined raw sugar

½ teaspoon fine sea salt, or to taste

Cooked rice, cilantro leaves, sautéed spinach + flatbreads, to serve

+ Soak chilies in hot water for 5–10 minutes. Drain, halve, and remove as many seeds as you can before roughly chopping. Blend in a food processor with the cumin seeds and garlic to form a rough paste (alternatively, chop all the ingredients very finely with a sharp knife or use a mortar and pestle).

+ Heat ghee or oil in a large heavy-bottomed frying pan over medium heat, add tofu cubes, and lightly brown on all sides for 8–10 minutes. Lift out tofu to a plate and add chili paste, tamarind puree, tomato paste, curry leaves, asafoetida, sugar, and salt to the pan. Cook, stirring often, for 3–4 minutes until thick and fragrant. Add tofu and ¾ cup (185 ml) water, stirring well to coat, then simmer on low for another 5–8 minutes until sauce thickens and tofu heats through. Serve hot with basmati rice, a few cilantro leaves, sautéed spinach, and freshly cooked flatbread on the side.

NOTE: Tamarind puree can be bought, but I make my own from blocks of tamarind pulp; simply break off a chunk, rip it into little pieces, and add enough boiling water to just cover. Leave for 10–15 minutes, stirring occasionally to break up the pulp. Tip the lot into a sieve over a bowl and press the mixture through with a metal spoon, scraping tamarind puree off the underside of the sieve as you go. Discard the seeds. You want it to be about the same consistency as ketchup, so add a little extra water if needed. This can be stored in the fridge for 4–5 days or frozen in ice-cube trays. Once your block of tamarind paste is opened, store it in a ziplock bag in the fridge, where it will keep indefinitely.

SWEET + SOUR LEMONGRASS TEMPEH SERVES 4

Tamarind, with its naturally sweet and sour flavor, is a wonderful ingredient, and I always make sure I have some on hand. You can pick it up easily in solid block form at any good Asian or Indian grocer. If you are lucky enough to live somewhere where tamarind trees grow (we are currently growing our own from seed here in Australia, but fear it will be another 10 years before we see them big enough to produce pods), you can enjoy the fruit as a snack. Just crack open the pod, pull off the hairy-looking fibers, and eat, remembering to spit out the seeds.

2 tablespoons tamarind puree (see NOTE on page 140)

⅓ cup (80 ml) water

2–3 tablespoons virgin coconut oil

300 g package of tempeh, cut in half lengthwise + thinly sliced

1 small onion, thinly sliced

2 garlic cloves, finely chopped

1 tablespoon finely grated ginger

1 stalk lemongrass, white part only, finely chopped (see NOTE)

2 tablespoons muscovado or coconut sugar or soft brown sugar

1 tablespoon gluten-free soy sauce

Cooked rice, sliced bird's eye chilies, cilantro, and Thai basil leaves, to serve

+ Combine tamarind puree with ⅓ cup (80 ml) water and stir until fully incorporated.

+ Heat 1–2 tablespoons coconut oil in a frying pan over medium-high heat. Add tempeh (perhaps in two batches, depending on the size of your pan) and fry for 2–3 minutes each side until golden. Transfer to a plate, wipe out the pan with paper towel, and add another 1 tablespoon of coconut oil. Stir-fry onion, garlic, ginger, and lemongrass for 2–3 minutes until tender and golden.

+ Return tempeh to the pan along with the sugar, tamarind liquid, and soy sauce. Cook, stirring, until liquid has reduced to a glaze and is coating the tempeh. Season to taste with sea salt and ground white pepper and serve with jasmine rice, chopped chilies, and herbs.

NOTE: Keep the green tips of the lemongrass for making tea (simply steep in boiling water). You can finely chop the white part in bulk and freeze for later use.

PIZZA WITH CHILI GREENS, BOCCONCINI + OLIVE SALSA SERVES 4

I always know I'm onto a winner when my (wheat-, meat- + dairy-loving) husband gives a dish the thumbs up. When I first started converting pizza recipes to gluten-free, I used gums to try to hold it all together, with mixed results. Now I use the more natural psyllium husks to do a similar job. The added bonus being that the husks give the dough the same elasticity as wheat-based. You can fold these slices of pizza in half without cracking or crumbling. For completely vegan pizza, simply omit the bocconcini topping (I bet you'll find that you don't even miss the cheese with that lovely saltiness coming from the olive salsa anyway). The crusts can be cooked, cooled, and frozen flat, but I've found that the texture changes after freezing and they become much more breakable. They're so quick and easy to make fresh that I tend to do so each time.

pizza crust
2 teaspoons (7 g package) dried yeast
2 teaspoons unrefined raw sugar or honey
1¼ cup (310 ml) warm water
2 tablespoons extra-virgin olive oil
2 teaspoons apple cider vinegar
1 cup (140 g) fine brown rice flour
⅔ cup (110 g) potato flour
½ cup (70 g) buckwheat flour
1 tablespoon psyllium husks
1 teaspoon fine sea salt

toppings
1 tablespoon olive oil
2 garlic cloves, roughly chopped
1 long red chili (cayenne or Thai), thinly sliced
4 large handfuls spinach leaves
1 recipe tomato + basil sauce (page 234), or 2 cups of your favorite pizza sauce
7½ ounces (220 g) bocconcini (small mozzarella balls), roughly torn

olive salsa
½ cup (80 g) kalamata olives, pitted + finely chopped
2 tablespoons roughly chopped basil
1 tablespoon capers, finely chopped
1 tablespoon extra-virgin olive oil
2 teaspoons lemon juice
Freshly ground black pepper, to taste

+ Combine yeast, sugar, and 1¼ cups (310 ml) warm water in a bowl, cover with a tea towel, and let ferment for 5 minutes until foamy. Add olive oil, cider vinegar, brown rice, potato, and buckwheat flours, psyllium husks, and salt and whisk to form a thick smooth batter. Cover with a plate and set aside in a warm spot for 20–30 minutes.

+ Preheat oven to 400°F (200°C). Line two large baking sheets with parchment paper. Divide the pizza dough into four portions and put two on each tray. Using oiled hands (I find it easiest to have a small bowl of olive oil nearby), press and shape each portion of dough into a 7- to 8-inch round. The dough is quite sticky and not like regular pizza dough so just be patient and work to get it to a thickness of no more than ¼ inch. Once you have all four pizza crusts spread out, set aside for 15–20 minutes to proof. Bake for 10–15 minutes until partially cooked but not colored.

+ Meanwhile, for toppings, heat a frying pan over medium-high heat and add olive oil, garlic, and chili. Cook, stirring, for 30 seconds until fragrant before throwing in the spinach. Stir-fry for 1 minute or until just wilted. Season well with sea salt and black pepper. Spread tomato + basil sauce over pizza crusts and scatter with a little of the wilted spinach mixture and torn bocconcini. Bake for another 18–20 minutes or until the crust is golden and the cheese melted.

+ To make olive salsa, combine all the ingredients in a small bowl and spoon over pizzas just before serving.

CHICKPEA FALAFEL WRAPS WITH TAHINI YOGURT + RED ONION RELISH SERVES 4

Best not to attempt this one on a busy school night, but if you have time to spare on the weekend or are looking to impress your friends, this is your dish. I sprout my chickpeas first, making them much easier to digest, so allow a couple of days for this. But, of course, the falafels can be made the traditional way using chickpeas that have been soaked overnight. If you don't have time to make the buckwheat tabouli, a few slices of tomato and some finely diced cucumber scattered over the tahini yogurt will do the trick.

1 cup (180 g) dried chickpeas, soaked for 24 hours in plenty of cold water

2 tablespoons cumin seeds, lightly toasted + ground

2 teaspoons coriander seeds, lightly toasted + ground

½ red onion, roughly chopped

2 garlic cloves, roughly chopped

1 long red chili (cayenne or Thai), finely chopped (deseeded if you like)

½ cup roughly chopped flat-leaf parsley

¼ cup roughly chopped cilantro

¼ cup roughly chopped mint

¾ teaspoon fine sea salt

½ teaspoon gluten-free baking powder

1–2 teaspoons chickpea (chana or besan) flour, if needed

Ghee or olive oil

Buckwheat tabouli (page 82), flatbreads (page 242) + natural plain yogurt, to serve

tahini yogurt

½ cup (125 ml) natural plain yogurt

2 tablespoons tahini

Juice of ½ lemon

1 small garlic clove, crushed

red onion relish

1 red onion, very finely sliced

1 long red chili (cayenne or Thai), thinly sliced

¼ cup roughly chopped flat-leaf parsley

Extra-virgin olive oil

+ To sprout chickpeas, drain them well, rinse, and drain again. Transfer to a glass jar, place a square of muslin over the top, and secure with an elastic band—if you have a sprouting bag or nut milk bag, use this instead. If using a jar, lay on its side with something propping the bottom up slightly, allowing any excess water to drain off; if using the bag, simply lay flat on its side on a tea towel or hang it over the sink. Leave at room temperature out of direct sunlight for 2–3 days, making sure you rinse and drain the sprouts every 12 hours until they are about ½-inch long. Rinse well and drain, then lay out flat on a tea towel to dry a little before continuing with the recipe.

+ If you are not sprouting your chickpeas, drain the soaked chickpeas well and lay out on a tea towel to dry a little (this ensures your falafel mixture is not too wet and you hopefully won't need to add any chickpea flour to the mix).

+ Place sprouted/soaked chickpeas, spices, onion, garlic, chili, herbs, salt, baking powder, and a good few grinds of black pepper in a food processor. Blend on high, scraping down the bowl at least once, until finely ground. A little bit of mixture squeezed should hold together loosely; if not, add 1–2 teaspoons chickpea flour and blend. Don't be

tempted to add any more than this or your falafel will be doughy (ideally you don't want to have to add any flour). Cover and set aside in the fridge while you prepare everything else. (Make tabouli and flatbreads now, if you are using.)

+ To make tahini yogurt, mix all ingredients until smooth and season well. To make red onion relish, mix onion with a good few pinches of fine sea salt, using your hands to break onion into single pieces. Set aside for 20 minutes to soften and mellow. Add chili, parsley, and a good drizzle of oil.

+ Shape tablespoons of falafel mixture into small patties, aiming to get around 16. Heat a little ghee or oil in a large frying pan over medium heat and pan-fry falafel (in batches if necessary) for 2–3 minutes on each side until golden brown and heated through. Place a generous dollop of tahini yogurt onto each flatbread and spread down the center. Top with a few spoonfuls of tabouli, three or four falafel, a little plain yogurt, and red onion relish.

WARM LENTILS WITH SWEET + SOUR CABBAGE + PARSLEY SALAD

SERVES 4–6

All too often lentils play only a minor role or find themselves served as a side dish. I've long been a fan of making them the star, whether in a salad or a more substantial dish like this one. You need to source Puy-style lentils here, the small green French lentils that hold their shape when cooked. The true Le Puy lentils, from the French town of the same name, cost a fortune and can be hard to track down. It's now relatively easy to find the same lentils sold under the name "French-style" or "Puy-style." Beluga (black lentils) are a great alternative if you can't find Puy-style.

2 cups (400 g) Puy-style lentils, rinsed

1 large onion, finely diced

4 garlic cloves, peeled but left whole

2 thyme sprigs

2 bay leaves, fresh or dried

6 cups (1½ liters) cold water

Juice of 1 lemon

3 tablespoons extra-virgin olive oil

sweet + sour cabbage

2 tablespoons olive oil

½ red cabbage (approx. 1½ pounds), cored + finely shredded

1 onion, finely sliced

1 teaspoon fennel seeds

⅓ cup (80 ml) red wine vinegar

¼ cup (50 g) unrefined raw sugar

parsley salad

1½ cups loosely packed flat-leaf parsley

½ red onion, very finely sliced

Juice of ½ lemon

2 tablespoons extra-virgin olive oil + extra to drizzle

+ Place lentils, onion, garlic, thyme, and bay leaves into a saucepan with 6 cups (1½ liters) cold water. Bring to a boil, then reduce to a simmer and cook for 25–30 minutes or until the lentils are tender and water absorbed (timing will depend on how fresh your lentils are, so add more water if needed). Discard thyme and bay leaves and drain off any excess liquid. Lightly mash the garlic into the lentils, adding lemon juice and extra-virgin olive oil, and seasoning to taste with sea salt and black pepper. Cover to keep warm.

+ Meanwhile, to make the sweet and sour cabbage, heat oil in a large saucepan over medium heat, add cabbage, onion, and fennel seeds, and cook, stirring constantly, for 2–3 minutes until the cabbage is just starting to wilt. Add vinegar and sugar, reduce heat to low, cover with a lid, and cook for 10 minutes, stirring occasionally. Remove lid, increase heat slightly, and cook for another 15–20 minutes, stirring occasionally, until all liquid is absorbed and cabbage is tender and sweet. (Keep checking during those last few minutes as it has a tendency to stick to the pan and burn.) Season to taste with sea salt and black pepper.

+ To make salad, combine parsley, red onion, lemon juice, and extra-virgin olive oil. Place a scoop of lentils onto each plate, top with a generous dollop of cabbage and a scattering of parsley salad. Serve warm, not piping hot.

RED LENTIL DHAL SERVES 4

I love to explore the aisles of my local Indian grocer and I have a huge array of pulses in my pantry to try out, but it is still the humble red lentil that I choose for making dhal. I occasionally use split red lentils and split chana dhal (split chickpeas) to add texture. Look for the Indian bay leaf—similar in appearance to the common bay leaf but with a mild cinnamon flavor—or just pop a cinnamon stick or a pinch of ground cinnamon in with the lentils as they cook. I use whole cumin seeds, which I toast and finely grind myself. Although it's not imperative, and you can use preground, I strongly suggest you get into the habit of grinding your own, as the flavor is incomparable. A cheap little mortar and pestle works great for small amounts of spices.

1 cup (180 g) red lentils, rinsed

1 Indian bay leaf

Small pinch of asafoetida, optional

4 cups (1 liter) cold water

2 tablespoons ghee or virgin coconut oil

1 onion, finely diced

2 garlic cloves, finely chopped

1 long green or red chili (cayenne or Thai), deseeded + finely chopped

2 teaspoons cumin seeds, lightly toasted + finely ground

1 teaspoon ground turmeric

2 teaspoons garam masala

1 teaspoon fine sea salt

1 stem of fresh curry leaves, stalk discarded, optional

Cooked white or brown basmati rice, cilantro leaves, and flatbread (page 242), to serve

+ Place red lentils, bay leaf, asafoetida, and 4 cups (1 liter) cold water in a saucepan. Bring to a boil, then reduce heat and simmer for 20–25 minutes until lentils are soft and have collapsed. Skim off any foam that rises to the surface during cooking.

+ Meanwhile, heat ghee or oil in a small frying pan over medium heat, add onion, and cook, stirring often, for 8–10 minutes until very tender and golden brown. Don't be tempted to skimp on this stage: it's the caramelized onion that gives this dhal its beautiful rich flavor. Add garlic and chili and cook for another 1–2 minutes. Stir in the cumin, turmeric, garam masala, salt, and curry leaves and cook for 1 minute or until fragrant. Add spice mix to lentils and simmer for 10 minutes, adding more water if necessary to thin, or cooking for longer to thicken. Serve with basmati rice, cilantro, and freshly cooked flatbreads.

HARISSA SQUASH + FETA GALETTE SERVES 4–6

I love the combination of fiery harissa paste, golden roasted squash, and salty feta in this light and flaky free-form tart. I serve it with Arugula, Pear + Almond salad (page 90) for an all-out autumn feast. We grow our own Queensland blue squash—and they're perfect here—but butternut squash is good and widely available, too. (You just need a squash that keeps its moisture when roasted and doesn't dry out.) The harissa can be stored in the fridge for a few days, and the piecrust overnight, if you want to prepare some steps in advance.

Approx. 2 pounds crown, Queensland blue, or butternut squash, peeled + chopped into 1-inch chunks

½ cup harissa (page 230) + extra, to serve

1 recipe savory piecrust (page 224)

3 ounces (80–100 g) feta cheese, crumbled

1 egg yolk mixed with 2 teaspoons rice milk or almond milk

Cilantro leaves, to serve

+ Preheat oven to 350°F (180°C) and lightly grease a baking sheet. Combine squash and harissa in a large bowl, mixing to thoroughly coat. Turn out onto the baking sheet and roast for 30–35 minutes, turning a few times during cooking, until tender and golden. Set aside to cool completely.

+ Roll out piecrust on a lightly rice-floured surface or between two sheets of parchment paper to roughly 12-inch round and ⅛-inch thick. Place on a baking sheet and top with the roasted squash, leaving a 2½-inch border. Crumble feta over the top, then fold edge of the pastry to make a raised crust. Brush piecrust with egg wash and bake for 40–45 minutes until crust is crisp and golden. Serve hot or at room temperature, scattered with chopped cilantro leaves and with extra harissa on the side.

LENTIL SPAGHETTI SERVES 3–4

Whenever I make my tomato + basil sauce in late summer/early autumn, I make it in bulk and stir cooked lentils into half the batch before freezing in dinner-sized portions. And, if you forget to defrost (as I so often do), you can put in a saucepan still frozen, add a touch of water, cover the pan, and heat it up gently. This is the simplest version of my lentil spaghetti, but I often sauté onion and garlic with any other vegetables that are hanging around and stir that into the sauce as well.

¼ cup (50 g) Puy-style lentils, rinsed

1 tablespoon finely chopped thyme

2 teaspoons dried oregano

1 tablespoon capers, roughly chopped

12 kalamata olives, pitted + roughly chopped

1 recipe tomato + basil sauce (page 234) or 2 cups of your favorite pasta sauce

Pinch of dried chili flakes, optional

8-ounce (250 g) package gluten-free spaghetti

Extra-virgin olive oil, to drizzle

Basil or flat-leaf parsley, roughly torn, to serve

+ Place lentils, thyme, and oregano in a saucepan, cover with plenty of cold water, and bring to a boil. Reduce heat to a simmer and cook for 20–25 minutes until tender. Drain off excess water. Put capers, olives, sauce, drained lentils, and chili flakes in a saucepan and simmer for 5–8 minutes until warmed through.

+ Meanwhile, bring a large saucepan of salted water to a boil and cook spaghetti for 8–10 minutes until cooked through but still firm to the bite. Drain and drizzle generously with extra-virgin olive oil. Serve with sauce and a scattering of herbs.

TOFU NOODLE SOUP SERVES 4

If you travel through Vietnam, you'll see crowds of people sitting around roadside vendors, eating huge bowls of steaming hot broth with noodles, beef, and piles of fresh herbs. Walking past the bowl-slurping goodness that is Vietnamese phở made me want to eat meat for the first time in my life. Having stood next to my mother-in-law as she works in the kitchen for up to two days making the stock and then the broth, and seeing how much love and attention goes into the traditional beef version, I knew my vegetarian effort would have to be good if I was to honor such an amazing dish. Making phở is all about the layering and depth of flavor, so the list of ingredients and method may seem a tad long, but I can assure you that every spice, vegetable, and step has its purpose. And the end result will be worth every single moment of your time, I promise.

8-ounce (185 g) package dried flat rice noodles
Olive oil
12-ounce (350 g) package firm tofu, cut into ½-inch slices
1 onion, finely sliced
½ cup roughly chopped cilantro
2 tablespoons finely chopped chives
2 limes, cut into wedges
2 handfuls mung bean sprouts
Sliced bird's eye chili
Thai basil leaves
gluten-free hoisin sauce

stock
¼ cup (20 g) coriander seeds
6 whole cloves
2 black cardamom pods, bruised (see NOTE)
1 cinnamon stick
2 star anise
2 slices dried licorice root (see NOTE)
1 teaspoon black peppercorns
1 teaspoon fennel seeds
1 whole long red chili (cayenne or Thai)
1 onion, unpeeled + quartered
2-inch piece of ginger, unpeeled + sliced
3 garlic cloves, bruised but unpeeled
2 carrots, ends trimmed + cut into 4 pieces
2 celery stalks, cut into 4 pieces
3 spring onions, chopped in half
½ cup (125 ml) Shaoxing cooking wine or dry sherry (see NOTE)
2 tablespoons gluten-free soy sauce
2 tablespoons unrefined raw sugar or grated pure palm sugar
8 cups (2 liters) cold water
1 tablespoon fine sea salt, or to taste

+ To make stock, lightly toast all the spices in a dry frying pan for 1–2 minutes until fragrant. Arrange onion, ginger, and garlic on a baking sheet and char under the broiler for 6–8 minutes or until slightly blackened, turning occasionally to char on all sides. Place spices, blackened onion, ginger, and garlic, and remaining stock ingredients, except salt, in a large stockpot with water. You can tie the spices in a small piece of muslin or spice bag, but I just toss them right in. Bring to a boil, reduce to a simmer, and cook uncovered for 1 hour. Strain through a fine sieve or piece of muslin and return to very low heat to keep warm without reducing any further. Add salt to the strained stock, to taste.

+ Meanwhile, soak rice noodles in boiling water for 10–15 minutes or until pliable. Drain well. Heat a little oil in a frying pan and panfry tofu for 3–4 minutes on either side until golden. Remove from the pan and, when cool enough to handle, slice each piece into long strips. Mix together onion, cilantro, and chives in a bowl. Arrange bowls of lime wedges, mung bean sprouts, sliced chili, Thai basil, and hoisin sauce on the table for everyone to serve themselves. When ready to serve, bring stock back to a full boil. Spoon noodles into deep serving bowls, cover with boiling stock and scatter with a handful of tofu slices, some onion mixture, and a handful of mung bean sprouts. Encourage each person to add as much lime juice, chili, hoisin, and Thai basil leaves as they like. Any broth left over can be frozen for up to 3 months.

NOTE: You can find these ingredients at your local Asian grocer. Regular green cardamom can be used in place of black if necessary. Licorice root is sold in small bags, looks like little dried pieces of wood chips, smells of licorice, and gives a lovely sweet anise flavor to this soup. Shaoxing (also known as Shao hsing) is a Chinese cooking wine made from glutinous rice, yeast, and water (and sometimes wheat). It is cheap and adds a lovely depth of flavor and can be splashed on stir-fries, too. If you are celiac or very sensitive to gluten and can't find Shaoxing that doesn't contain wheat, dry sherry can be used in its place.

STUFFED PEPPERS WITH QUINOA, SPINACH + FETA SERVES 4

My mum makes a seriously good spanakopita. It was always taken to family Christmas parties for us vegetarians, and we'd polish off a whole large pie in a matter of minutes. I've had to say farewell to phyllo pastry since going gluten-free, but it was always the flavor of the filling that I enjoyed most anyway. So, I've used those spanakopita flavors here, along with a little bit of quinoa to fill the banana peppers. Instead of making the sauce, you can use my tomato + basil sauce recipe (page 234).

filling

2 tablespoons olive oil
1 onion, finely diced
2 garlic cloves, finely chopped
1 teaspoon dried oregano
3 big handfuls of spinach leaves
1½ cups cooked quinoa (you'll need to cook ½ cup quinoa for this amount)
Small handful of basil leaves, roughly chopped
½ cup (55 g) crumbled feta cheese
1 large free-range egg, lightly beaten
8 large banana peppers/chilies, or 4 small hot peppers, halved

sauce

3 tablespoons extra-virgin olive oil
2 garlic cloves, finely chopped
14-ounce (400 g) can chopped tomatoes
1–2 teaspoons unrefined raw sugar
Small handful of basil leaves, roughly chopped

+ Heat olive oil in a large frying pan over medium heat. Add onion and cook, stirring often, for 3–4 minutes until tender. Add garlic and oregano and cook for another minute until fragrant. Add spinach and cook until just wilted. Remove from heat, stir in quinoa, basil, and feta, and season to taste with plenty of sea salt and black pepper. Set aside to cool for 5 minutes before stirring in the beaten egg.

+ Lay peppers on the cutting board. Decide which way they all like to sit and then, using a sharp knife, make a slit through the top of each one lengthwise, taking care not to cut through to the bottom. Gently open up the peppers just enough to scoop out the seeds with your fingers, then rinse them out with cold running water.

+ Preheat oven to 350°F (180°C).

+ To make sauce, heat oil in a large ovenproof frying pan (cast iron is perfect here) that's big enough to fit all the peppers snugly. Add garlic and cook gently over medium heat until fragrant but not colored. Add canned tomatoes, sugar, and season to taste with sea salt and black pepper. Bring sauce to a boil and then reduce heat to a simmer and cook, stirring occasionally, for 4–5 minutes or until reduced slightly. Remove from heat and stir in basil leaves.

+ Meanwhile, stuff peppers with about ¼ cup of filling each. Do your best to stuff it right down into very tip of each pepper. Arrange the peppers on top of the sauce (if you don't own an ovenproof frying pan, transfer to a baking dish) and bake for 40–45 minutes or until peppers are tender and filling cooked through. Serve stuffed peppers with a good scoop of that lovely sauce and salad on the side.

DRINKS + FROZEN GOODNESS

It's perhaps strange, considering how many years I've spent working in cafés, but I've never been a drinker of coffee or regular tea.
These days it's also very rare for me to drink alcohol, other than the
odd glass of cider (friends who knew me in my late teens will be
laughing in disbelief at that). So, beyond these obvious associations
with the word "drinks," there are actually myriad choices that are
liquid by nature and equally as delicious. In this chapter you'll also
find some of my favorite frozen treats—these are usually enjoyed
in high rotation around our house throughout the long and ridiculously hot summer months here in Perth.

ALMOND MILK MAKES APPROX. 3 CUPS (750 ML)

You can sweeten almond milk with a few soaked dried dates or a little brown rice syrup or pure maple syrup; leave unsweetened for use in savory recipes. To make vanilla cashew milk, use cashews in place of almonds and add a touch of vanilla paste or extract before blending.

1 cup (150 g) whole raw almonds, soaked overnight in cold water

3 cups (750 ml) cold water, divided

2 tablespoons brown rice syrup, pure maple syrup, or two soaked dried dates, optional

+ Drain the almonds well, rinse, and transfer to a blender. Add 1 cup (250 ml) cold water and a good pinch of sea salt and blend on high for 30–45 seconds or until a reasonably smooth paste forms.

+ Add 2 cups (500 ml) cold water and the sweetener (if using), and blend for another minute or until smooth. If you own a high-powered blender, you can blend all the ingredients in one batch.

+ If you have a nut milk bag, use this to strain the milk into a large measuring cup or carafe, otherwise line a large sieve with a piece of muslin or cheesecloth (when I first started making nut milk I used one of the muslin wraps we had from when the kids were babies) and place the sieve over a bowl. Strain the milk through the muslin (you may need to do this in 2–3 batches depending on how big your cloth is), and then bring up the sides of the cloth gently, trying not to let any pulp escape. Hold all four corners firmly and squeeze as much milk as you can out of the cloth. Leftover almond pulp can be mixed into porridge, sprinkled over muesli, added to bread dough, or fed to your worm farm or compost bin. Serve the milk immediately or transfer to a glass jar and store in the fridge.

+ The milk will keep for 3 days in the fridge, but shake well before serving as some of the solids will naturally settle down to the bottom.

WALNUT + MAPLE MILK MAKES APPROX. 4 CUPS (1 LITER)

When I first started making my own nut milk I went on a bit of an almond-milk bender. I couldn't get enough of the stuff, and I'd stand in the kitchen, guzzling glass after glass, with mounds of almond pulp piling up around me. However, I'm not a huge fan of walnuts, so when my little brother Louie asked if I'd tried making walnut milk, I was a bit dismissive. It was only when he mentioned pairing it with maple syrup that my ears pricked up and I gave it a go. To my surprise, I became a walnut convert. Walnut milk tastes of walnut, but at the same time it doesn't. The essence of walnut is there, but so mildly that you wonder where all that walnut-iness went.

1 cup (140 g) raw walnuts, whole or pieces, soaked overnight in cold water

3 cups (750 ml) cold water, divided

2 tablespoons pure maple syrup

+ Drain the walnuts well, rinse, and transfer to a blender. Add 1 cup (250 ml) cold water and a good pinch of sea salt and blend on high for 30–45 seconds or until a reasonably smooth paste forms. Add 2 cups (500 ml) cold water and the maple syrup and blend for another 1 minute or until smooth. If you own a high-powered blender, you can blend all the ingredients in one batch.

+ If you have a nut milk bag, use this to strain the milk into a large measuring cup or carafe, otherwise line a large sieve with a piece of muslin or cheesecloth and place the sieve over a bowl. Strain the milk through the muslin (you may need to do this in 2–3 batches depending on how big your cloth is), and then bring up the sides of the cloth gently, trying not to let any pulp escape. Hold all four corners firmly and squeeze as much milk as you can out of the cloth. Leftover walnut pulp can be mixed into porridge, sprinkled over muesli, added to bread dough, or fed to your worm farm or compost bin. Serve the milk immediately or transfer to a glass jar and store in the fridge.

+ The milk will keep for 3 days in the fridge, but shake well before serving as some of the solids will naturally settle down to the bottom.

PLUM LASSI SERVES 4–6

Back home in New Zealand there was a Black Doris plum tree that we used to raid every year, filling supermarket shopping bags full of deep crimson goodness. No one else ever picked them, and they'd have only been eaten by the birds otherwise. Then word got out and the rest of the town zeroed in, and after that we were lucky to get a handful of plums from that tree. I struggled to find a plum here in Australia that even came close to the Black Doris, but keep a look-out in high summer when the blood plum varieties such as Satsuma or Mariposa come into fruit.

1 pound (500 g) Black Doris or other red-fleshed plums, pitted and halved

2 tablespoons honey or brown rice syrup + extra, to taste

2 cups (500 g) natural plain yogurt

1 cup ice

2 teaspoons rose water, optional

+ Place plums, honey, and a splash of water in a saucepan. Cover and cook over medium heat, stirring occasionally, for 8–10 minutes or until plums are tender. Remove from the heat and set aside until completely cold (these will keep for up to 3 days in the fridge in a glass jar or container).

+ Place plums and their syrup, yogurt, ice, a couple of extra spoonfuls of honey/brown rice syrup, and rose water (if using) into a blender and blend on high for 30–60 seconds or until creamy. Serve immediately.

PEPPERMINT + LEMON BALM TEA

Peppermint is well known for its ability to soothe tummies and help with digestion, while lemon balm is a great natural relaxant and helps promote a good night's sleep. This is more an idea than a recipe, and it came about one afternoon when I was visiting my mum. Mum never has a whole lot of spare cash, but she knows how to make something out of nothing and has one of the most productive vegetable gardens around. Instead of offering me the usual tea or coffee, she went out front to some peppermint and lemon balm plants that were growing up through the cracks in the path and plucked off a handful or two. She put the leaves in mugs and topped them up with boiled rainwater.

Per serving
Sprigs of fresh peppermint
Sprigs of fresh lemon balm
Honey or brown rice syrup,
    to taste

+ Place peppermint and lemon balm in a cup and pour in boiling water. Set aside and steep for 2–3 minutes before removing leaves and enjoying hot. I drink mine unsweetened, but you can add a touch of honey or brown rice syrup, to taste.

SPICED HOT CHOCOLATE SERVES 4

Ground cashews are used in Indian cooking to help thicken sauces and curries. This idea got me thinking that they might also work as the base for a lusciously creamy, spiced hot chocolate. As you heat the milk, you'll see its viscosity change, but don't be tempted to boil it or you'll end up with chocolate sauce (although that's not always a bad thing). I like to remove it from the heat just before it comes to a boil, but you can thin it down with a little extra almond milk if you accidentally take things too far. If you like the flavor even richer, you can add another tablespoon of cocoa. You can pick up raw cashews at your local Indian grocer where they are much cheaper than at a supermarket. Keep a lookout there for cashew pieces too, which are even cheaper still. They are perfect to use in recipes like this where they all just get blended up anyway.

1 cup (125 g) raw cashews, soaked overnight in cold water

4 cups (1 liter) water

3 tablespoons cocoa powder

3–4 tablespoons pure maple syrup, brown rice syrup, or muscovado sugar, to taste

1 teaspoon vanilla extract

½ teaspoon ground cinnamon

⅛–¼ teaspoon ground cayenne pepper, or to taste

almond milk, to thin, if needed

+ Drain the cashews well, rinse, and transfer to a blender with 4 cups (1 liter) water. Blend on high for 30–60 seconds until smooth. If you have a nut milk bag, use this to strain the milk into a large measuring cup or carafe, otherwise line a large sieve with a piece of muslin or cheesecloth (when I first started making nut milk I used one of the muslin wraps we had from when the kids were babies) and place the sieve over a bowl. Strain the milk through the muslin, you may need to do this in 2–3 batches depending on how big your cloth is, and then bring up the sides of the cloth gently, trying not to let any pulp escape. Hold all four corners firmly and squeeze as much milk as you can out of the cloth. Leftover pulp can be mixed into porridge, sprinkled over muesli, added to bread dough or fed to your worm farm or compost bin.

+ Combine remaining ingredients and a good pinch of fine sea salt with ½ cup (125 ml) of the cashew milk in a saucepan and whisk to form a smooth paste. Add remaining cashew milk and whisk over medium heat until slightly thickened and hot but not boiling. The longer you heat the milk, the thicker it will become (you can thin it down with a little almond milk, if needed).

GINGER KEFIR WATER MAKES 4 CUPS (1 LITER)

For a description of the benefits of kefir water, see page 24. I flavor mine with fresh ginger during the brewing process, but you can also add berries or fruit once the grains are strained out, then seal and leave overnight in the fridge before drinking. Kefir grains are pretty forgiving things; however, they don't like coming into contact with metal. So make sure you use a glass jar to brew and plastic spoons and sieve to strain. A pinch of Himalayan salt crystals will add minerals, and a small pinch of baking soda increases alkalinity (which water kefir prefers).

2 cups (500 ml) water

2–3 tablespoons unrefined raw sugar

1–2 tablespoons natural raisins or a few pieces of other organic, oil- and sulfate-free dried fruit

2–3 slices ginger

Pinch of Himalayan salt crystals, optional

Small pinch of baking soda, optional

¼ cup water kefir grains

Mint leaves and slices of lime, to serve, optional

+ Place 2 cups (500 ml) water in a clean 1 liter glass jar and mix in sugar, raisins, ginger, salt, and baking soda, if using. Stir to slightly dissolve the sugar. Add the water kefir grains and top up with enough water to fill the jar. Screw on lid and leave sitting at room temperature, out of direct sunlight, for 24–48 hours or until most of the raisins have risen to the top (you will see and hear lots of bubbles, too).

+ Place a plastic sieve over a bowl or wide-necked bottle and pour the entire contents of the jar into it, discarding the raisins and ginger. The resulting fizzy amber drink is ready to consume, or, if you want to further increase its nutritional content, you can leave it for another 1–2 days in the fridge (but just be warned that a small amount of alcohol is produced and the longer you leave it the stronger it gets). I drink mine immediately with mint and a squeeze of lemon or lime juice, as it loses its fizz unless stored in an airtight manner.

ICED DANDELION TEA SERVES 4

Dandelion tea was something my mum and dad used to drink. It was their "coffee" in a near coffee-less world, and I seem to have developed the same taste for this hugely nutritive tea. In winter I like my dandelion piping hot, with a touch of honey to sweeten its naturally bitter taste and a dash of almond milk (most other dairy-free milks have a tendency to separate). But this is my summer version, full of milky goodness and lots of ice.

8 teaspoons (or 4 teabags) dandelion root tea

1 cup (250 ml) boiling water

3 tablespoons honey or brown rice syrup

2 cups (500 ml) almond milk

2 cups ice + extra, to serve, if you like

+ Stir together dandelion tea, boiling water, and honey and set aside until cold. Strain and pour into a blender with the almond milk and ice. Blend on high until smooth and creamy. Serve over extra ice, if you like.

GINGER NECTAR SERVES 4–5

While I was living in Byron Bay, I fell in love with a locally made drink called ginger nectar. Its refreshing coolness was very welcome after a long and ridiculously hot shift in the kitchen I was running. It was a sweet drink, but not in-your-face so, with a good bite of gingeriness that left me wanting more than the little bottles held. For a few years after we left Byron I forgot about it, but when I was feeling nauseous beyond belief and trying to get through long days in a hot kitchen during my first pregnancy, it was ginger nectar that came to the rescue. Nausea + ginger = good. Every morning I'd mix up a little bit of syrup and top it up throughout the day with a glass of chilled sparkling water.

If you don't like the heat of the ginger, reduce it to 2 tablespoons or even less. I like to use a mild floral honey that won't overpower the lemon and ginger.

¼ cup (60 ml) mild honey, such as clover or wildflower

2 tablespoons boiling water

¼ cup (60 ml) lemon juice

2–2½ tablespoons fresh ginger juice (see NOTE)

Ice cubes + still or sparkling water, to serve

+ Stir together honey and boiling water until honey has melted. Add lemon and ginger juice and mix well. Store in a glass jar in the fridge for 3–4 days. To serve, pour 3–4 tablespoons of syrup into each glass, add a few ice cubes, and top up with still or sparkling water.

NOTE: You will need a large piece of ginger, approx. 2 to 3 ounces (60–80 g), to give you 2–2½ tablespoons of ginger juice. Use a juicer, or finely grate the ginger and squeeze with your hands into a sieve set over a bowl to extract as much juice as you can.

WATERMELON, ROSE WATER + MINT ICEPOPS MAKES 6

I once worked with a woman who performed wonders as a naturopath during the day and moonlighted as a waitress by night. Running that kitchen was one of the most stressful jobs I've ever had, and I often felt overwhelmed by the madness. There was one little thing she did that perked us all up and helped ease the pain: most nights during service, right when we needed it the most, she would give us a very simple little glass of juice— freshly juiced watermelon with lemon, mint, and a good dash of rose water.

I don't know the science behind it, but I find that watermelon juice tends to separate less if blended and passed through a fine sieve, as opposed to using your juicer. You will get some separation when it freezes, but much less with the blender.

3 cups (approx. 500 g)
  diced watermelon
¼ cup (60 ml) brown rice
  syrup or 3 tablespoons
  unrefined raw sugar
¼ cup (60 ml) lemon juice
2 teaspoons rose water
½ cup mint leaves

+ Place all the ingredients in a blender and blend on high for 20–30 seconds or until smooth. Transfer to a sieve set over a bowl and using a metal spoon pass the mixture through, trying to get out as much of the liquid as possible. Discard pulp. Pour into icepop molds, snapping on the lids; if you are using wooden sticks, place the molds in the freezer for 1–2 hours until partially frozen before inserting sticks. Freeze for at least 4–5 hours or overnight. To serve, run the molds briefly under warm water to loosen the icepops.

STRAWBERRY + THAI BASIL SORBET SERVES 4–6

You have probably noticed that I like to add herbs to most of my sweet treats. The addition of Thai basil here provides just enough gently peppery anise-like flavor to keep people guessing, and will have them coming back for more. If Thai basil is not readily available where you live, it's super-easy to grow yourself. If all else fails, use regular sweet basil.

2 pounds (1 kg)
  strawberries, hulled
  + cut in half if large
1 cup (200 g) unrefined
  raw sugar
1 cup loosely packed Thai
  basil leaves, roughly
  torn
½ cup (125 ml) lemon juice

+ Stir together strawberries and sugar in a large bowl and set aside for 1–1½ hours, stirring occasionally until syrupy. Drain syrup from the berries into a small saucepan and add basil. Bring to a boil and boil for 1 minute. Remove from the heat and set aside to infuse, cooling down to room temperature.

+ Puree strawberries in a blender until smooth, then pass through a fine sieve set over a large bowl to remove most of the seeds (some seeds will sneak through, but that's okay). Strain basil syrup over strawberry puree, using your hands to squeeze every last bit of flavor from those basil leaves. Add lemon juice and stir before covering and chiling in the fridge for at least 2 hours or overnight. Churn in an ice-cream maker for 20–25 minutes or follow the manufacturer's instructions. Transfer to a container and freeze for another 2 hours until a bit firmer.

+ If you don't have an ice-cream maker, pour the mixture into a shallow freezer-proof container (a loaf pan is perfect), freeze for 1 hour until the edges are starting to freeze, and then beat with a whisk until smooth. Return to the freezer and repeat this 2–3 times before leaving to freeze for 2 hours. The results won't be quite the same, but still delicious.

BANANA BERRY ICE CREAM SERVES 4

Back before this became a worldwide health trend, we simply knew it as ice cream. My mum would make a summery treat of frozen bananas, soy milk, and honey. Nowadays I like to add some berries to counteract the natural sweetness of the banana, or you can try mango in their place. Since I try to limit the amount of soy we eat, I use a touch of coconut milk or yogurt to help move things along in the food processor. You will need to start this the night before if you don't already have bananas in your freezer.

2 ripe bananas, peeled +
   cut into 1-inch rounds
2 cups (250 g) mixed
   frozen berries
¼ cup (60 ml) coconut milk
   or natural plain yogurt +
   extra as needed

+ Place banana pieces on a tray in a single layer and freeze overnight. Just before serving, place the frozen banana slices, frozen berries, and coconut milk or yogurt into a food processor and pulse until starting to break up. Scrape down the side of the bowl and then blend on high until a smooth, creamy ice cream forms. You can add a touch more milk/yogurt to help it process better, but remember that the more liquid you add, the softer the end result will be. Scoop into bowls and serve immediately. This ice cream doesn't refreeze well, but it's fast and easy to put together if you have the fruit pre-frozen, so making it fresh shouldn't be a problem.

HOKEY POKEY ICE CREAM SERVES 4–6

I love eating ice cream, but I possibly love making it even more. When I worked in Sydney, we used to churn it out by the liter most days, and I was often seen staring into the distance, daydreaming about owning a little ice-cream parlor. These days I always have two very happy little customers lined up with spoons to sample any ice cream that comes out of our kitchen. This slightly healthier version of this sponge toffee classic is often requested as "the one with caramel chunks in it, Mum."

3¼ cups (800 ml) coconut milk

2 tablespoons gluten-free organic cornstarch

½ cup (200 ml) almond or unsweetened rice milk

½ cup (100 g) unrefined raw sugar

2 tablespoons brown rice syrup

1 teaspoon vanilla extract

hokey pokey

4 tablespoons blended unrefined raw sugar

2 tablespoons golden syrup

1 teaspoon baking soda

+ Mix a few tablespoons of coconut milk with the cornstarch in a small bowl to form a smooth slurry. Pour remaining coconut milk into a saucepan with the almond milk, sugar, brown rice syrup, vanilla, and a good pinch of fine sea salt. Bring to just below boiling point. Whisk in cornstarch slurry and simmer for 1–2 minutes until slightly thickened. Remove from the heat, partially cover with a lid to prevent a skin forming, and set aside to cool. Strain through a fine sieve into a clean bowl, cover, and chill in the fridge for at least 2–4 hours or overnight.

+ To make hokey pokey, grease a metal tin with a little coconut oil. Put sugar, golden syrup, and 1 teaspoon water into a saucepan and heat gently, stirring until the sugar has melted. Increase heat and boil for 2–3 minutes, without stirring, until deep golden. You can swirl the pan a few times during cooking to make sure it's caramelizing evenly. Remove from heat, count to 10, and then whisk in the baking soda. As it foams up, quickly pour into the greased tin, scraping the side of the pan with a metal spoon. Let it cool and firm up for around 20 minutes. Once firm, use the end of a wooden spoon to smash it into small pieces, keeping in mind that it will melt somewhat once combined with the ice cream, so keep some pieces quite chunky. Store, airtight, until needed.

+ Churn the custard base in an ice-cream maker for 20–25 minutes or following the manufacturer's instructions, adding the hokey pokey pieces for the last few minutes of churning. Eat immediately or transfer to a container and freeze for 2 hours to firm up further before serving. If it remains in the fridge for longer than 2 hours and gets too firm, simply leave on the counter for 15–20 minutes to soften slightly.

+ To make without an ice-cream machine, transfer the custard to a shallow freezer-proof container (a loaf pan is perfect), freeze for 1 hour until the edges are starting to freeze, and then beat with a whisk until smooth. Return to the freezer and repeat this 2–3 times before folding in the hokey pokey pieces and leaving to freeze for 2 hours. The results won't be quite the same, but still delicious.

CHOCOLATE CREAM POPS MAKES 5

When you bite into these it's hard to believe they contain no dairy whatsoever. The creamy chocolate filling is reminiscent of the infamous Kiwi ice-block we used to eat as kids, but these are made with ingredients more nutritious than most breakfast cereals! If you want to take these one step closer to the original, dip the ends in melted chocolate before serving.

1 cup (125 g) raw cashews (see NOTE)
1 cup (160 g) pitted dried dates
¼ cup (15 g) cocoa powder
1 cup (250–300 ml) coconut milk
1–2 tablespoons pure maple syrup, optional

+ Place cashews and dates in separate bowls, cover with cold water, and soak at room temperature overnight (or in the fridge in hot weather). Drain and transfer to a blender. Add cocoa powder, coconut milk, and a pinch of fine sea salt and blend until smooth. Start with 1 tablespoon of maple syrup, then taste, adding more if you like—the mixture should taste pretty sweet at this stage as the freezing dulls the sweetness a little. Spoon into icepop molds, snap on lids, or press in wooden sticks and freeze overnight. Pull out of the freezer 5 minutes before serving to soften slightly, then run the outside of the mold under warm water to release the icepops.

NOTE: You can pick up raw cashews at your local Indian grocer much cheaper than from a supermarket. Cashew pieces are cheaper still and perfect to use in recipes like this where they just get blended up anyway.

MANGO LIME SLUSHIE SERVES 4

The house we live in has not one, but two huge Kensington mango trees in the backyard. When we were looking for somewhere to rent, the choice came down to two houses. One had a dishwasher but no fruit trees, while the other had no dishwasher, but two mango trees and one lemon tree. It was an easy choice even if there have been many moments during recipe testing for this book when I've thought I was mad for passing up the dishwasher! If having a mango tree in your backyard is not an option, buy cheap mangoes in summer and freeze the flesh in chunks for making smoothies, ice cream, or slushies. Frozen mango flesh tastes just like sorbet and can be eaten in chunks, blended to make a naturally sweet frozen treat, or thinned down a touch with orange juice for a refreshing icy drink.

2 large ripe mangoes, roughly chopped

Juice of 2–3 limes (or lemons), to taste + zest, to serve, optional

1 cup (250 ml) freshly squeezed orange juice + extra if needed

+ Place mango pieces in a single layer on a flat plate or tray and freeze for at least 4–5 hours until frozen. Transfer to a blender, add lime and orange juice, and blend on high until smooth, creamy, and icy. Add a little more orange juice if your blender is struggling. Serve immediately.

SWEETNESS

There's no point lying about it: I have a pretty serious sweet tooth. Often a piece of fruit, a bowl of yogurt, or a fresh Medjool date is enough to satisfy it at the end of a meal. But occasionally I find myself daydreaming about crumbles, tarts, and cakes.

Most of the desserts I make don't feature an overload of sugar, especially since I've had kids. I think an occasional treat is an important part of life, but usually I stick with raw-inspired desserts and those that are sweetened with unrefined sugars or natural alternatives—if only to justify having seconds!

CHOCOLATE AVOCADO TART SERVES 10–12

A chocolate tart made from nothing but raw ingredients that I ate sitting on the grass at Byron Bay's monthly market is what sparked my interest in alternative desserts. Here was a tart that tasted of rich chocolate, had the texture of a smooth mousse, but was healthier than a bowl of muesli! Where could I sign up for more?

I've adapted this recipe from one given to me by my good friend Grace. I sometimes add a little orange zest to the base and brown rice syrup can be used instead of maple—just add an extra tablespoon as it's not quite as sweet. Please don't be lulled into thinking that this is a great way to use up old, overripe avocados—been there, done that! Use creamy, perfectly ripe avocados. I buy mine hard and leave them on the counter to ripen naturally. It takes a little longer but you are guaranteed no stringy bits (a telltale sign that they've been stored in the fridge at some point).

crust

1½ cups (240 g) pitted dried dates

2 cups (180 g) dried coconut

filling

2 cups (320 g) pitted dried dates

3 medium avocados, perfectly ripe

½ cup (30 g) cocoa powder

¼ cup (60 ml) virgin coconut oil, melted if solid

2 tablespoons pure maple syrup

¼ teaspoon fine sea salt

+ Place the two quantities of dried dates into two separate bowls (making a mental note of which is which!), cover with warm water, and leave for 20 minutes until softened. Drain the dates for the crust first, squeezing to extract as much water as you can. Place in a food processor with the coconut and mix until finely chopped and starting to form one large mass. Press into a round 10-inch loose-bottomed cake pan (line with parchment paper if preferred, but I don't find it needs it), pressing the mixture firmly over the bottom with the back of a spoon and about 1½ inches up the side. Refrigerate while you prepare the filling.

+ To make the filling, wipe out the food processor (no need to get finicky), drain the remaining dates, and squeeze out any excess water. Place into food processor with the avocado flesh, cocoa, coconut oil, maple syrup, and sea salt. Pulse until lightly blended, scraping the bowl down a couple of times as you go. When the mixture is starting to blend more freely, blend on high for 2–3 minutes (scraping the bowl a few times) until fairly smooth. There may still be a few lumps of date but they will soften up later, so don't worry.

+ Spread filling over the base and smooth with the back of a spoon. Chill for at least 4 hours, preferably overnight, before using a warm knife to slice into small portions. Keeps for up to 5 days, airtight, in the fridge.

BLACKBERRY, APPLE + HAZELNUT CRUMBLE SERVES 4–6

I could eat crumble every night, I love it that much. One winter, many moons ago, my friends and I went through a phase of devising mad and wonderful variations for this classic (that's what you do to keep entertained in small-town New Zealand . . .), but this simple combination of apples and blackberries, with a little crunch of toasted hazelnuts and a zip of orange, has always been my favorite. I like to use a combination of two different apples so that some pieces collapse completely while others remain intact, adding texture. I don't tend to sweeten my fruit base, but you can add 1–2 tablespoons unrefined raw sugar or honey when you stew the apples. Leftover crumble makes a great breakfast served cold with a dollop of plain yogurt.

2 large Granny Smith apples, peeled, cored + sliced

2 large Pink Lady apples, peeled, cored + sliced

Finely grated zest + juice of 1 orange

½ teaspoon ground cinnamon

1½ cups (185 g) blackberries, fresh or frozen

crumble topping

⅔ cup (80 g) whole hazelnuts

½ cup (70 g) fine brown rice flour

½ cup (55 g) ground almonds

5 tablespoons (70 g) cold butter, chopped into small cubes

⅓ cup (65 g) muscovado or soft brown sugar

+ Preheat oven to 350°F (180°C). To make crumble topping, spread hazelnuts on a baking sheet and roast for 6–8 minutes or until golden, shaking the tray once to ensure even baking. Transfer to a clean tea towel, rub off as many of the skins as you can, then roughly chop.

+ Put flour, ground almonds, and butter in a bowl. Use your hands to rub in the butter until it resembles coarse breadcrumbs and the mixture clumps together into small pieces when squeezed (it will feel a little more moist than regular crumble topping at this stage). Stir in sugar and toasted hazelnuts.

+ Meanwhile, for the filling, put sliced apples, orange zest, juice, and cinnamon into a saucepan, cover with a lid, and bring to a boil over high heat. Reduce to a simmer and cook for 8–10 minutes, stirring occasionally until apple is tender. Transfer to a 2 quart oven dish and top with blackberries. Scatter with some of the crumble mixture and then squeeze the rest of the crumble together with your hands to form large clumps before gently scattering over top.

+ Bake for 40–45 minutes or until the top is golden brown and the filling bubbling up over the crumble in places. Serve warm with vanilla ice cream or natural plain yogurt.

GOLDEN PAVLOVA WITH WHIPPED COCONUT CREAM + MANGO SERVES 8

There was no way I could write a cookbook without including a recipe for pavlova, the lovely meringue-based dessert invented by us Kiwis! Ownership politics aside, Kiwis and Aussies seem to agree that it's one of our all-time favorites. I use natural unrefined sugar, which gives it a beautiful golden hue. No pavlova is complete without a pile of whipped cream on top and I've used softly whipped coconut cream here if you need a dairy-free alternative. We always have mangoes kicking around in the summer, but you can top this with whatever seasonal fruits you like.

1 tablespoon gluten-free organic cornstarch

2 teaspoons apple cider vinegar

1 teaspoon vanilla extract

6 large free-range egg whites, at room temperature

1½ cups (300 g) firmly packed blended unrefined raw sugar

Two 14-ounce (400 ml) cans coconut milk, chilled overnight (see NOTE)

Honey, maple syrup, or powdered sugar, to taste

1 large mango, thinly sliced

1–2 small kiwi, thinly sliced

2–3 passion fruit

✛ Preheat oven to 250°F (120°C). Line a large baking sheet with parchment paper. Mix together cornstarch, cider vinegar, and vanilla extract to form a smooth slurry. Whisk eggwhites with electric beaters for 3–4 minutes until stiff peaks form. Gradually add the sugar, a tablespoon at a time, beating well after each addition until stiff and glossy (this should take around 4–5 minutes). Rub a little bit of mixture between two fingers and you should feel no grittiness. Beat in cornstarch slurry. Transfer to tray and shape the mixture into an 8-inch circle. Bake for 1½ hours, turn off the oven, and leave pavlova in oven to cool completely, overnight if possible (while you chill your coconut milk). Pavlova can be stored, airtight, at room temperature for up to 5 days before filling.

✛ Open the cans of chilled coconut milk. Scrape off the solid top layer of "cream" from both cans and place into a clean bowl. Reserve the watery liquid from the bottom for another use (add to your morning porridge in place of milk or use in smoothies). Whisk the cream for 1–2 minutes with electric beaters or a balloon whisk, until thick like regular whipped cream. Sweeten to taste with a touch of honey, maple syrup, or powdered sugar, keeping in mind that the pavlova is sweet. Pile onto the pavlova, arrange mango and kiwi slices on top, and drizzle with passion fruit pulp. Serve immediately.

NOTE: For the whipped coconut cream you may have to experiment with different brands of coconut milk to find out which ones set firm in the fridge, as not all do. Refrigerate the can overnight and then give it a gentle shake. If you don't hear any movement in the can, you should be good to go. If there is movement, reserve that can for another use and try a different brand. I find AROY-D brand works well—it is made in Thailand and found at your local Asian grocer.

CHAI "CHEESECAKE" WITH EARL GREY FIG SAUCE SERVES 12 OR MORE

I've always steered clear of gelatine-set cheesecakes and, while I do really love making baked cheesecakes, when it comes to eating them, I find there's just too much, well, cheese! When I first tried a slice of raw cheesecake at a café here in Perth, I was blown away by the creaminess and texture of the filling. If you are lucky enough to own a high-powdered blender, you can whip this up easily and the filling will be silky smooth. However, if like me you only own an old cheapy, just take it slow and maybe blend in batches to prevent the poor motor from burning out. You can use whole cashews or cashew pieces—both can be picked up from your local Indian grocer much cheaper than at the supermarket. I prefer to use fresh whole spices and grind them myself with a small mortar and pestle or a spice grinder too. But I've also provided the ground equivalent, so you really have no excuse not to make this!

crust
1½ cups (240 g) pitted dried dates, roughly chopped
⅔ cup (100 g) whole raw almonds
1 tablespoon virgin coconut oil

filling
3 cups (375 g) raw cashews, soaked overnight in cold water + drained
¾ cup (185 ml) virgin coconut oil, melted if solid
½ cup (125 ml) lemon juice
½ cup (125 ml) pure maple syrup
1 teaspoon vanilla extract
¼ teaspoon fine sea salt
Seeds from 20 cardamom pods (¾ teaspoon ground)
6 whole cloves (½ teaspoon ground)
½ teaspoon fennel seeds (½ teaspoon ground)
½ teaspoon black peppercorns (just over ¼ teaspoon ground)
2 teaspoons ground ginger
1 teaspoon ground cinnamon

Earl Grey fig sauce
¾ cup (185 ml) boiling water
2 Earl Grey tea bags
½ cup (85 g) firmly packed sliced dried figs
Juice of ½ lemon
1 tablespoon pure maple syrup

Fresh figs, to serve, optional

+ To make the crust, line the base and side of a 10-inch loose-bottomed cake pan with parchment paper. Place dates, almonds, and coconut oil in a food processor and blend on high until finely ground. Press mixture into the base of the tin, using the back of a spoon to pack down firmly.

+ To make filling, place drained cashews, coconut oil, lemon juice, maple syrup, vanilla, and salt in a blender and set aside for a minute. Finely grind the whole spices with a mortar and pestle or spice grinder. Add to the blender along with the ground ginger and cinnamon. Blend on high until smooth. You may need to help things along a little by stopping occasionally and giving things a stir. Pour over the crust and smooth the surface. Place in the freezer for 2–3 hours or until set (you can also chill overnight in the fridge if preferred, but I like mine semi-frozen around the edges). Cheesecake slices will store in a covered container in the freezer for up to 1 month. Remove from the freezer 20–30 minutes before serving to allow to soften.

+ To make Earl Grey fig sauce, combine boiling water, tea, and figs in a small glass bowl or jug, pressing the figs down to fully submerge, and leave until cool. Remove and discard tea bags, squeezing them to extract as much flavor as you can. Transfer to a blender, add lemon juice and maple syrup, and blend on high until smooth. Serve cheesecake with a drizzle of Earl Grey fig sauce and fresh figs, if in season.

DARK CHOCOLATE, ORANGE + ROSEMARY TRUFFLES MAKES 24

At work, years ago, I used to make a biscotti that was jam-packed full of flavor and contained chocolate, orange, black pepper, and rosemary. I know, it sounds weird. But when you taste those flavors, you'll quickly realize that they just work together. These lovely rich dairy-free truffles are a nice thing to have hanging around in the fridge for whenever the chocolate urge arises. I use a 50% dark chocolate in the filling as I find anything higher becomes too much when paired with the coconut milk.

½ cup (125 ml) coconut milk

Finely grated zest of 1 orange

1 teaspoon finely chopped rosemary, + extra, to dust

¼ teaspoon freshly ground black pepper

8½ ounces (250 g) dark chocolate, chopped roughly

7 ounces (200 g) dark chocolate, melted

+ To make truffles, combine coconut milk, orange zest, rosemary, black pepper, and a good pinch of fine sea salt in a saucepan. Bring to a boil briefly, then remove from heat and add chopped chocolate. Cover with a lid and set aside for 2–3 minutes, then whisk until smooth. Set aside for 3–4 hours until mixture has set (you can place it in the fridge to speed things up or if you are making it in hot weather).

+ Use a hot spoon (dip it in a mug of boiling water) to scoop teaspoonfuls of mixture and roll into balls. This will get messy, but you can lick your hands afterwards! Chill again for a little bit if they are starting to melt. Using two forks, dip the balls into melted chocolate, letting the excess run off before transferring to a parchment-lined baking sheet. Dust each with a little chopped rosemary as you go. Set aside until cooled. Can be kept, covered, in the fridge for up to 1 week, but I like them best when they've sat out on the counter for at least 30 minutes to soften slightly before eating.

ALMOND MILK PUDDING WITH CHERRY ROSE COMPOTE SERVES 4–6

I make the most of the brief cherry season by buying them in bulk and turning them into compote, or simply removing the pits and freezing in ziplock bags for later on in the year. I make my own almond milk (page 162) at a fraction of the cost of store-bought—for a recipe like this, I reckon it's well worth the extra effort and will reward you with a beautiful rich creamy pudding.

Ground rice can be found at your local health food store or baking section of the supermarket. It's a little more coarsely ground than white rice flour and often used to make rice porridge for babies. Rose water is available at Indian grocers and specialty food stores. The cherry rose compote is equally good with plain yogurt or spooned over pancakes or crepes and will happily keep in the fridge for 3–4 days if you feel like making extra.

¼ cup (25 g) gluten-free organic cornstarch

⅓ cup (60 g) ground rice

⅓ cup (65 g) unrefined raw sugar

1 teaspoon vanilla bean paste or vanilla extract

4 cups (1 liter) almond milk (page 162)

2 teaspoons rosewater

¼ cup (40 g) pistachio nuts, roughly chopped

cherry rose compote

14 ounces (400 g) pitted cherries (2 generous handfuls of fresh cherries)

Juice of ½ lemon

2 tablespoons unrefined raw sugar

2 tablespoons water

2 teaspoons rose water

+ Mix cornstarch, ground rice, sugar, and vanilla with just enough of the almond milk to form a thick slurry. Pour remaining almond milk into a saucepan and bring to a boil. Whisk in the cornstarch mixture and cook for 1 minute or until thick, whisking constantly to prevent it sticking to the bottom. Remove from heat and add rose water. Pour into 4–6 small bowls or glasses and let cool, before chilling in the fridge for 2 hours or overnight. Serve topped with cherry rose compote and a sprinkling of chopped pistachios.

+ To make the cherry rose compote, combine cherries, lemon juice, sugar, and 2 tablespoons water in a small saucepan, bring to a boil, reduce to a simmer, and cook for 5–6 minutes or until cherries are tender and liquid has reduced to a light syrup. Remove from heat and stir in rose water. Set aside to cool. Can be stored in the fridge for 3–4 days.

STICKY BLACK RICE + BEANS WITH SALTED COCONUT CREAM SERVES 4–6

One of the things I love most about Vietnamese desserts is their use of beans. In the Western world we tend to only use beans in savory dishes, but they add such a lovely mellow earthiness to sweets that it seems a shame. My mother-in-law makes the most amazing desserts: some using sticky white rice with black-eyed beans; others with split yellow mung beans cooked with sugar and coconut cream. I love the deep nutty flavor of black rice and have taken a hint from my mother-in-law to serve it with lightly salted coconut cream. You can find packages of frozen pandan leaves at your local Asian grocery store, or just leave it out and use 1 teaspoon vanilla bean paste or extract instead.

1½ cups (220 g) black glutinous rice, rinsed + soaked overnight in plenty of cold water + drained

1 pandan leaf (fresh or frozen) tied in a knot

2½ cups (560 ml) water

14-ounce (400 ml) can coconut cream

¼ teaspoon fine sea salt

½–⅔ cup (60–85 g) grated pure palm sugar or unrefined raw sugar

1 cup (115 g) cooked drained black beans (see NOTE)

Fresh fruit, toasted sesame seeds + coconut flakes, to serve

+ Combine rice, a pinch of sea salt, pandan leaf, and 2¼ cups (560 ml) water in a saucepan and bring to a boil. Cover with a tight-fitting lid and reduce the heat to as low as it can go. Cook covered for 45 minutes.

+ Meanwhile, to make salted coconut cream, reduce the coconut cream in a small saucepan over medium heat for 4–5 minutes, stirring until slightly thickened. Add ¼ teaspoon of fine sea salt—you should be able to taste the salt without it being overly salty.

+ Remove the rice from the heat and discard pandan leaf. Stir in the palm sugar to taste and add the black beans. Spoon into serving bowls and cool completely, or mold in small cups and turn out just before serving. Spoon a little salted coconut cream around portions of black rice and top with sliced fruit, toasted sesame seeds, and coconut flakes. I like to serve both the sauce and the rice pudding at room temperature, but you can also serve the sauce warm.

NOTE: If using dried black beans you will need about ½ cup dried non-heat-treated black beans. Soak overnight in plenty of water, drain, and cover with fresh water. Bring to a boil, then reduce and simmer for about 50 minutes or until beans are tender but not falling apart. Drain well. Any excess cooked beans can be frozen in ziplock bags for later use. In a pinch you can use a 14 ounce (400 g) can of black beans, but make sure you drain and rinse them very well before using.

STRAWBERRY LEMON THYME TARTS WITH HONEY LABNEH MAKES 6

I like to make these tarts at the peak of strawberry season when their natural sweetness is as intense as their color. If you're short on time, the labneh and compote are perfect on their own as a light summer dessert. You will need to start this recipe the night before to give the labneh time to drain. If you are in a hurry, simply use thick Greek yogurt or mascarpone instead. If you don't have small tart pans, you can make one large tart instead. The piecrust is very tender and crumbly, so expect a fair amount of breakage when you slice the large one. Use regular thyme if lemon thyme is unavailable.

almond piecrust

1¼ cup (175 g) fine brown rice flour

¼ cup (25 g) tapioca flour or organic gluten-free cornstarch

¾ cup (80 g) ground almonds

¼ cup (50 g) firmly packed blended unrefined raw sugar

8¾ tablespoons (125 g) cold butter, cubed

½ cup (75 g) toasted almonds, finely chopped

1 large free-range egg

strawberry lemon thyme compote

1 pound (500 g) strawberries, hulled + cut in half if large

Finely grated zest + juice of 1 lemon

2 tablespoons unrefined raw sugar, or to taste

1 tablespoon finely chopped lemon thyme

1 teaspoon cornstarch mixed with 1½ teaspoons cold water

honey labneh

1 recipe labneh (page 222) or 2 cups thick Greek yogurt

2 tablespoons honey

+ Grease six 4¾-inch loose-bottomed tart pans. To make piecrust, place flours, ground almonds, and sugar into a food processor and pulse a few times to evenly distribute. Add the butter and pulse until the mixture resembles coarse breadcrumbs. Add the chopped almonds and pulse a few more times to slightly break them down (mixture should still be fairly chunky). Add egg and pulse until the dough just comes together. Turn out onto a rice-floured workspace, knead a few times, and shape into a flat disc. Cover and chill for 30 minutes in the fridge.

+ Divide dough into 6 portions. Roll out on lightly rice-floured parchment paper until about ⅛- to ¼-inch thick—this will be a slightly strange task as there are big lumps of almonds in there, but do your best. Line the pans with piecrust, gently pressing in the edges with your fingers. If the crust tears, simply patch it together, then trim the tops neatly (any spare pastry can be baked into cookies). If you find lining the pans frustrating, you can just press the dough into the tins with your fingers—you won't have even piecrust, but it will taste just as good. Use a fork to prick a few holes in the bottom of each tart. Chill tart pans in freezer while you preheat the oven to 350°F (180°C).

+ To make compote, put the strawberries, zest, juice, sugar, and thyme into a saucepan. Cover and cook over medium heat for 2–4 minutes until the berries just start to break down and release some of their juice. Taste and add more sugar if needed (if your berries are not overly ripe or your lemons very tart, you may need more sweetness). Add cornstarch mixture and, stirring constantly, cook for 30–45 seconds or until thickened slightly. Remove from the heat and cool.

+ In a medium-sized bowl, stir honey into the labneh. Remove tart crusts from the freezer and bake for 18–20 minutes until crisp and lightly golden. Remove from the oven and set aside to cool completely. To assemble, carefully turn out tart crusts onto serving plates (they are delicate so do take care). Spoon honey labneh into each crust and top generously with strawberry thyme compote. Serve immediately.

APRICOT TARTS WITH KAFFIR LIME SUGAR MAKES 6

Summer stone fruits are so wonderful that I find myself not wanting to muck around with them too much. They are the star of these very simple fresh fruit tarts. The Kaffir lime sugar adds just enough intrigue, but lemon or lime zest also works if Kaffir lime leaves aren't available. Because the tarts have a tendency to soften, they are best eaten straight from the oven. If you don't think you will eat them all immediately, only cook what you will eat and freeze the remainder once you've put in the apricot slices. Bake them straight from the freezer for 35–40 minutes. Peaches or nectarines can be used in place of the apricots.

1 recipe sweet piecrust (page 226)

5 Kaffir lime leaves, stems removed

1½ tablespoons unrefined raw sugar

¼ cup (25 g) ground almonds

12 apricots, pitted + finely sliced

+ Preheat oven to 350°F (180°C). Grease six 4¾-inch loose-bottomed tart pans. Make piecrust and chill, then divide into six even portions. Roll out each piece between sheets of lightly rice-floured parchment paper until around ⅛-inch thick. Peel off the top sheet and use bottom sheet to help invert the pastry into the pan, pressing in gently with your fingers. Trim excess dough from the top and patch up any tears with scraps. Chill for 10 minutes while you make the kaffir lime sugar.

+ Very finely shred two of the kaffir lime leaves. Pound remaining leaves and raw sugar into a fine green powder with a mortar and pestle or spice grinder. Remove tart crusts from the fridge, scatter 2 teaspoons ground almonds over the base of each, and arrange apricot slices neatly in each pan (freeze at this stage if you're going to). Sprinkle a little Kaffir lime sugar evenly over each tart and scatter with shredded leaves. Bake for 30–35 minutes or until the pastry is golden and apricots are tender. Let cool in pan for 5 minutes before turning out and serving immediately. Lovely with a scoop of vanilla ice cream or softly whipped cream.

FLOURLESS DARK CHOCOLATE CARDAMOM CAKE SERVES 10–12

This gorgeous cake towers high above the pan as you remove it from the oven, but then, right before your eyes, all the life deflates out of it. Don't be alarmed—that's exactly how it's supposed to behave! Being completely flourless, this cake is light and almost mousse-like at room temperature, but if you like things a little more intense, chill it in the fridge for a while and watch it become dense and fudgy. Serving this without some version of cream is not an option in my book!

8½ ounces (250 g) dark chocolate, chopped roughly

8¾ tablespoons (125 g) butter, cubed

3½ tablespoons (50 ml) orange juice (or super-strong espresso coffee)

4 large free-range eggs, separated

⅔ cup (120 g) firmly packed blended unrefined raw sugar

2 tablespoons cocoa powder, sifted

Seeds from 12 cardamom pods, finely ground (or ½ teaspoon ground cardamom if you must!)

Whipped cream or whipped coconut cream (page 196), to serve

Fresh berries, to serve, optional

+ Preheat oven to 350°F (180°C). Grease and line the base and side of an 8-inch springform cake pan. Place chocolate, butter, and orange juice (or espresso) in a saucepan and heat gently, stirring, until melted and smooth. Remove from the heat and cool slightly. Beat yolks and half the sugar with electric beaters or a balloon whisk for 3–4 minutes until thick and pale. Fold in cooled chocolate mixture, cocoa powder, and ground cardamom.

+ Whisk egg whites in a clean bowl until stiff peaks form. Gradually beat in remaining ⅓ cup sugar, 1 tablespoon at a time, until you have a thick and glossy meringue.

+ Fold one-third of the meringue into the chocolate batter to loosen it (I was always taught that the first little bit of egg white is sacrificial, so don't be too concerned about folding in gently). Add the remaining meringue all at once and gently fold in with a spatula or large metal spoon in a cutting motion, turning the bowl around as you bring your spatula around the edge of the bowl and into the center. Stop folding the second you no longer see any white lumps of meringue and carefully transfer the batter to the tin, trying hard not to knock out any more air.

+ Bake for 35 minutes—it will look glorious and tower high above the pan, but will still jiggle slightly in the center.

+ Remove from the oven and let sit for 10 minutes, watching the life deflate out of it as it cools. Loosen the side of the pan and let cool completely. Serve at room temperature dusted with extra cocoa, or chill in the fridge for a few hours for a more fudge-like consistency. Serve with whipped cream or coconut cream and fresh berries, if you like. Cake will keep, airtight, in the fridge for up to 5 days.

MANGO + COCONUT JELLY MAKES 6

As a child, I loved Jell-O. It symbolized everything we were never allowed to eat at home: fluorescent coloring, gelatin, and sugar to the max. This recipe couldn't be further from the bright wobbly dreams of my youth. Made using only natural ingredients and set with agar, this coconut and mango jelly would make my mother proud. If you are new to agar, it is derived from seaweed and is a natural vegan alternative to gelatin. I buy mine in powder form from my local Asian grocery store where it's sold in small packages (be sure you buy plain agar as many packs are flavored and colored). You can also find it at health food stores. If you're using agar flakes instead of powder, you will need to use more than I've stated: 1 teaspoon powder equals 6 teaspoons flakes. To activate agar's setting properties, it must be boiled for a few minutes in the liquid and, unlike gelatin, it will set at room temperature. If you are unable to find fresh mangoes, look for the cans of sweetened mango pulp sold at Indian grocery stores and use 2 cups of pulp in place of the mango and sugar in this recipe.

coconut jelly

14-ounce (400 ml) can coconut milk
2 tablespoons unrefined raw sugar or finely grated pure palm sugar
¼ teaspoon fine sea salt
3 Kaffir lime leaves, roughly torn, or the zest of 1 lime or lemon
1 teaspoon agar powder

mango jelly

Flesh of 2 large mangoes
¼ cup (50 g) unrefined raw sugar or finely grated pure palm sugar
1½ teaspoons agar powder
1 cup (250 ml) water
Juice of 1 lime or small lemon
Basil flowers, to serve, optional

+ Rinse six 200 ml glasses or ramekins with water and set aside (this will stop the jellies from sticking). For coconut jelly, put coconut milk, sugar, salt, Kaffir lime leaves, and agar powder in a small saucepan. Bring to a boil, stirring constantly to dissolve the sugar and prevent the agar from sticking to the bottom of the pan where it naturally wants to settle. Boil for 1 minute then remove from heat and set aside to infuse for 5 minutes. Discard lime leaves and pour mixture into glasses. Set aside until cool and then place in the fridge for 30 minutes to set.

+ For mango jelly, puree mango flesh and sugar in a blender until smooth. Put agar powder and 1 cup (250 ml) water in a small saucepan and bring to the boil, stirring often to prevent sticking. Boil for 1 minute. Add mango puree, whisking well, and return to a boil briefly. Remove from the heat and stir in the lime juice. Remove glasses from the fridge and divide mango mixture evenly between glasses. Set aside until cool and then chill in the fridge for 30 minutes until firm.

+ Serve in the glasses, topped with finely shredded Kaffir lime leaves and basil flowers, if you like. (If you try to unmold agar jellies the layers tend to separate, so serve in the glasses.)

CHOCOLATE MOUSSE TART SERVES 10–12

When I was about eight, my class made a cookbook. It was brilliant, in a stapled-together, newsprint kind of way. Each child brought in one or two favorite family recipes, and the teacher typed them all up and made a copy for everyone to take home. It mainly featured classic 1980s New Zealand cuisine: fudge, banana cake, coconut ice, and chocolate cake. I don't remember noticing at the time that my recipe was different from everyone else's, but now I wonder what the rest of the class thought when they got to my contribution: Mum's famous Carob Ripple Cheesecake made with tofu, carob, and bananas. It probably did nothing to help me lose my hippie associations. But even tofu-haters can be converted when it's combined with chocolate. Just don't tell them the secret ingredient until the very last crumb has disappeared . . . which won't take long.

crust
2 cups (320 g) pitted dried dates
½ cup (75 g) whole raw almonds
¼ cup (15 g) cocoa powder
1 tablespoon virgin coconut oil, melted if solid

chocolate mousse
1¼ pounds (600 g) silken tofu, drained well
¾ cup (200 g) natural smooth peanut butter
3 tablespoons pure maple syrup
1½ teaspoons vanilla extract
7 ounces (200 g) dark chocolate, melted

+ Line the base and side of a 10-inch cake pan with parchment paper. Blend the crust ingredients and a pinch of fine sea salt in a food processor on high for 1–2 minutes or until finely ground and when you squeeze a little bit between your fingers it sticks together. Press into bottom of cake pan, using a spoon to compact firmly.

+ To make chocolate mousse, wipe out the bowl of the processor and blend tofu, peanut butter, maple syrup, vanilla, and a good pinch of fine sea salt until smooth and creamy. Stop to scrape down the side of the bowl a couple of times during blending. Add melted chocolate and blend for another 20–30 seconds until fully incorporated. Pour over base and spread with a spoon to smooth. Chill overnight to set and then cut into portions with a hot knife.

PECAN MAPLE TART SERVES 10

This is a naturally sweetened tart that highlights the flavors of pure maple syrup, crunchy pecans, and gorgeous buttery pastry. You could use walnuts in place of pecans for a slightly cheaper alternative. If blind baking is new to you, don't fear: it's a useful step when making tarts with wet fillings and ensures the crust stays crisp once cooked. I have a glass jar of cheap dried beans that I keep specifically to use as baking weights, but uncooked rice also works well.

1 recipe sweet piecrust
(page 226)
2 cups (185 g) pecans,
lightly toasted
¾ cup (185 ml) pure maple
syrup
2 large free-range eggs,
lightly beaten
2¾ tablespoons (40 g)
butter or ghee, melted
2 tablespoons fine brown
rice flour
Softly whipped cream or
thick plain yogurt, to
serve

+ Preheat oven to 350°F (180°C). Grease a 12½ x 4¾-inch loose-bottomed fluted tart pan or a 10-inch round loose-bottomed tart pan. Roll out piecrust to ⅛-inch thick between two sheets of lightly rice-floured parchment paper. Line tart pan with piecrust, patching up any tears with extra. Trim excess crust from the top and chill for 15–20 minutes. Place a piece of parchment paper over the shell, fill with baking beans or rice, and bake for 15 minutes. Remove paper and beans (the gluten-free dough is soft and may stick a little to the paper; just do your best to peel it off carefully and not pull up too much dough) and cook for another 5 minutes or until golden.

+ Scatter pecans over the piecrust base. Whisk maple syrup, eggs, butter, brown rice flour, and a good pinch of fine sea salt together until smooth. Pour over the pecans and bake for 20–25 minutes or until filling is just set. Cool in pan for 10 minutes before transferring tart to a wire rack to cool. Serve warm or at room temperature with cream or yogurt. This is best served on day of baking but will store, airtight, for 1–2 days.

ETC.

We all know that it's often the little touches that make a dish truly special: that chili-kissed sauce you can't stop eating, the strawberry jam with a touch of fresh thyme, or that flaky buttery piecrust you can't get enough of. In this chapter you'll find all the little things I make to keep mealtimes exciting, along with a bunch of homemade basics I couldn't live without.

YOGURT MAKES 4 CUPS (1 LITER)

Not all yogurts are good for you. Take a glance at the ingredients list of most mainstream supermarket yogurts and you'll find sugar as one of the first ingredients, along with all sorts of preservatives, colorings, thickeners, and quite often gluten. Real yogurt only needs 2–3 ingredients and is full of gut-friendly bacteria, calcium, and protein. My parents made our yogurt in an old glass canning jar, wrapped in a tea towel and set on top of the hot water heater to thicken overnight. My sister and I shared the room next to the hot water closet, so our job was to collect the warm jar in the morning and bring it downstairs for breakfast. Mum and Dad added a little milk powder to make it extra creamy, but the whole milk I use produces a lovely thick yogurt without any help. If you don't have a hot water heater handy, put the yogurt in a cooler with a few hot water bottles tucked alongside and cover the whole lot with a towel for added insulation. If you live somewhere warm, just let it sit out on the counter for a few hours. And always remember to save a few tablespoons to make your next batch.

4 cups (1 liter) whole milk
2 tablespoons milk powder (optional)
2 tablespoons plain live yogurt (any store-bought natural yogurt will do to start)

+ Pour the milk in a large saucepan, whisk in milk powder (if using), and bring to just below boiling point. As it starts to froth up and reach boiling point, remove from heat and set aside to cool for about 20 minutes. When it has cooled enough for you to hold your finger in for 10–15 seconds without burning, discard the skin from the surface of the milk. Put the plain yogurt into a 1 quart glass or ceramic jar, pour in a little of the warm milk, and whisk to dissolve yogurt before adding the rest and mixing thoroughly. Cover or put on the lid and keep in a warm place, undisturbed, for at least 6–8 hours or overnight (in cold weather it can take 12+ hours and if super-hot it can be done in 4–5 hours).

+ When ready, it should be spoonable, like thick custard. The longer you leave it the sharper the flavor will be. Transfer to the fridge for 2–3 hours or overnight, where it will thicken further as it cools. I do the opposite of my parents and make my yogurt in the morning, placing it in the fridge in the afternoon or before I go bed. It is lovely, thick, and ready to eat the following morning. It will keep in the fridge for up to 1 week. Always save 2 tablespoons of yogurt to make your next batch.

+ If you like a thicker Greek-style yogurt follow my instructions for making labneh (page 222), draining for just 2–3 hours until it reaches the thickness you want.

LABNEH

MAKES APPROX. 1½–2 CUPS (DEPENDING ON HOW LONG YOU STRAIN IT FOR)

Labneh is one of my favorite foods and something I make often. It's basically just strained yogurt and is sometimes known as yogurt cheese. You can buy it from specialty stores, but it's super-easy and cheaper to make yourself. If you use homemade yogurt (page 220) it becomes cheaper still. Eat it straight from the fridge with fresh fruit and a drizzle of honey, or roll into balls and eat as a savory snack. I use it in my strawberry lemon thyme tarts (page 206), in place of yogurt in my roasted rhubarb with orange yogurt (page 46), and to offset the sweetness of strawberry jam when spooned into choux puffs (page 118).

4 cups (1 liter) natural
plain yogurt

+ Combine yogurt with a pinch of sea salt. Spoon into a clean square of muslin or cheesecloth. Pull up all four corners of the cloth and tie. Hang it from a wooden spoon that is resting over a bowl or large plastic container (to collect the dripping whey). Leave in the fridge overnight or for up to 48 hours depending on how firm you want your labneh. Check the drip tray occasionally to make sure it's not overflowing. Reserve the whey: it freezes well and can be added to smoothies for an extra nutritional boost.

+ Remove labneh from the cloth. For a sweet labneh, stir in a little honey or sifted powdered sugar. For savory labneh, stir in some finely chopped herbs and season with sea salt and freshly ground black pepper. It can be eaten right away or savory labneh can be rolled into balls and put into a jar topped up with olive oil. The labneh balls will keep in the fridge for up to 2 weeks.

SAVORY PIECRUST MAKES ENOUGH TO LINE A 10-INCH ROUND TART PAN

I use this buttery flaky pastry for my harissa squash + feta galette (page 152), and also as a great base for quiche or pies. If you're not sure if your potato is large enough, cook 2 medium ones to be on the safe side. You can always eat the leftovers . . .

1 large potato, peeled +
   roughly chopped
⅔ cup (93 g) fine brown
   rice flour
½ cup (55 g) chickpea
   (chana or besan) flour
⅓ cup (35 g) tapioca flour
   or gluten-free organic
   cornstarch
½ teaspoon sea salt
8¾ tablespoons (125 g)
   chilled butter, cubed
1 large free-range egg yolk

+ Place potato in a small saucepan with a little sea salt, cover with water, and bring to a boil. Simmer for 10–15 minutes until soft. Drain, mash, and cool. You should have around ¾ cup of mashed potato. This can be done well in advance and stored overnight in the fridge in a covered container.

+ Place other dry ingredients in a food processor and pulse together. Add butter and pulse until mixture resembles fine breadcrumbs. Add cooled potato and egg yolk and pulse a couple more times until combined. Turn out onto a clean, lightly rice-floured countertop and bring together with your hands, kneading a couple of times to form a soft dough. Form into a disc, place in a plastic bag, and chill for 30 minutes before using. Can be kept in the fridge for 2–3 days or frozen for up to 3 months (defrost in the fridge overnight before using).

tips for making piecrust

- Use butter straight from the fridge or freeze butter and grate it into the mix
- Keep everything as cold as you can and work quickly.
- Use a food processor: it's a million times faster than rubbing in by hand and keeps things much cooler.
- If dough is too dry and not coming together, add 1 teaspoon of chilled water at a time. But don't be tempted to add too much: the dough should just hold together when squeezed between your fingers or your piecrust will be tough, not flaky.
- Rest pastry in the fridge for at least 30–60 minutes before rolling, to allow the flours to soak up the liquid and make it easier to work with.
- Roll out piecrust between sheets of parchment paper to help you lift it easily into the pan (if any pieces break, simply pinch back together).
- If piecrust is too soft to work with, or sticking to the paper, refrigerate or even freeze for a while still on the paper.

SWEET PIECRUST

MAKES ENOUGH TO LINE ONE 10-INCH ROUND TART PAN,
A 12½ x 4¾-INCH FLUTED TART PAN, OR SIX 4¾-INCH PANS

Making piecrust isn't difficult. Gluten-free dough is extra forgiving, as you don't have to worry about over-working the gluten (this can result in a tough texture when using wheat flour). If a little bit tears off when you're lining the pan, simply use a little extra dough to piece it back together. See tips for making piecrust on page 224.

1¼ cups (175 g) fine brown rice flour

¾ cup (80 g) ground almonds

¼ cup (25 g) tapioca flour or gluten-free organic cornstarch

¼ cup (50 g) firmly packed blended unrefined raw sugar

8¾ tablespoons (125 g) chilled butter, cubed

1 large free-range egg

+ Place brown rice flour, ground almonds, tapioca flour, sugar, and butter into a food processor and pulse until mixture resembles fine breadcrumbs. Add egg and pulse a couple more times until just combined. Turn mixture out onto a lightly rice-floured countertop and bring together with your hands, kneading a couple of times to form a soft dough. Form into a disc, place in a plastic bag, and chill in the fridge for 30 minutes before using. Can be kept in the fridge for 2–3 days or frozen for up to 3 months (defrost in the fridge overnight before using).

STRAWBERRY THYME JAM MAKES 6 JARS

I've always loved making jam and, when my children were babies, I used to sell it at our local markets. I buy cheap fruit at the end of summer and stock up the pantry, or give jars to friends as gifts throughout the year. This jam is lovely on pancakes, topped with softly whipped cream (a treat that instantly transports me back to my mother's kitchen), or sandwiched between crisp layers of choux pastry with labneh (page 118).

3¼ pounds (1.5 kg) strawberries, hulled + cut in half

6 cups (1.2 kg) unrefined raw sugar

Finely grated zest + juice of 1 large lemon

2 tablespoons finely chopped thyme leaves

+ Place a saucer in your freezer. Combine strawberries and sugar in a large wide heavy-bottomed saucepan and leave for 2 hours, stirring occasionally until syrupy. Add the rest of the ingredients and bring to a boil. Reduce to a rolling simmer and cook for 30–35 minutes until jam reaches setting point. To test, drop a little jam onto the chilled saucer, run your finger through the center, and if the jam doesn't run back into the center, it's ready. Pay close attention to the bottom of the pan in the last 5–10 minutes, making sure you stir often to prevent the jam from sticking. Pour into sterilized jars and seal with metal lids while hot. Will keep for up to 12 months in a cool dark place. Refrigerate once opened.

NOTE: To sterilize jars, wash well in hot soapy water, rinse, and dry in a preheated 250°F (120°C) oven for 30 minutes. Remove with tongs or a tea towel and fill with jam while piping hot. To sterilize lids immerse in boiling water for 5 minutes and handle with tongs.

HARISSA MAKES APPROX. 1 CUP

I love chilies, and one of my favorite ways to enjoy them is in this North African spice paste. Harissa is commonly used to flavor tagines, but it's also a lovely way to pep up eggs in the morning, stir through soups to give a final burst of flavor, or smear onto root vegetables before roasting. I use it in my harissa squash + feta galette (page 152), but once you've made it, you'll find yourself adding it to all sorts of dishes. If you like things hot, leave a few seeds in the chilies when you chop them.

1 large red bell pepper
Olive oil
5 dried chilies, soaked in boiling water for 10 minutes, drained, deseeded + roughly chopped
4 long red chilies, deseeded + roughly chopped
1 teaspoon cumin seeds, lightly toasted + ground
½ teaspoon fine sea salt
2 garlic cloves, roughly chopped
¼ cup (60 ml) extra-virgin olive oil

+ Preheat broiler to high. Place bell pepper on a baking sheet, drizzle with a little olive oil, and grill, turning often, for 8–10 minutes or until the skin on all sides is black and blistered. Place in a glass bowl, cover with a lid, and set aside for 5 minutes to sweat. Peel off the blackened skin and discard, along with the seeds.

+ Put roasted pepper and remaining ingredients except extra-virgin olive oil in a food processor or blender. If you have a mini food processor, now is the perfect time to use it as this small amount is quite tricky in a full-sized processor. Blend on high until smooth, stopping to scrape down the side a few times, until a paste forms. Add the olive oil and blend until emulsified. Check seasoning, adjust if desired, and transfer to a glass jar or container. Store in the fridge for up to 1 week.

FURIKAKE MAKES APPROX. 1¾ CUPS

If you're new to furikake, you've been missing out! One of our favorite family meals is crispy fried eggs over rice, sprinkled with a generous amount of furikake. This Japanese rice seasoning of sesame seeds and seaweed can be bought from your local Asian grocer; however, to avoid any added nasties, I prefer to make my own. I buy pre-shredded roasted nori from my local Asian grocer or supermarket, but you can shred sheets yourself with scissors. Any finely flaked seaweed can be used, but my personal favorites are flaked dulse or the beautifully colored karengo from New Zealand.

½ cup (60 g) raw hulled
    sesame seeds
1 tablespoon unrefined
    raw sugar
½ teaspoon fine sea salt
15 g package (approx.
    1 cup loosely packed)
    shredded roasted nori
¼ cup (10 g) flaked dulse
    or karengo seaweed

+ Place sesame seeds in a frying pan over medium-high heat and stir until just starting to color. Add sugar and salt and stir until seeds are light golden brown. Keep a close eye as they can go from golden to black in the blink of an eye, especially with the added sugar. Remove from the heat and transfer immediately to a large flat plate to cool.

+ Once cold, use a spoon or your hands to break up any clumps of sesame seeds, add shredded nori and dulse, and mix together. I like to get my hands in at this stage and scrunch it all to break up some of the shredded nori. Can be stored, airtight, for months and months.

TOMATO + BASIL SAUCE MAKES APPROX. 2 CUPS

If you peer into my freezer in late autumn, chances are you'll find stack upon stack of storage containers filled with this sauce in varying shades of red. This is what I use for my homemade pizza (page 144) and lentil spaghetti (page 154). If you buy boxes of cheap tomatoes at the markets or grow your own, double up the recipe or cook in batches of five as I do. You'll need to allow for a longer cooking time if you're making large batches.

¼ cup (60 ml) extra-virgin olive oil

1 red onion, finely diced

2 garlic cloves, roughly chopped

2 pounds (1 kg) tomatoes, cored, peeled + chopped (see NOTE)

1 teaspoon unrefined raw sugar

¼ cup roughly torn basil leaves

+ Heat olive oil in a large saucepan over medium heat, add onion, and sauté for 5 minutes, stirring often until soft. Stir in garlic and cook for another 1–2 minutes until fragrant. Add peeled and cored tomatoes, sugar, and a good few pinches each of salt and black pepper and simmer for 30–40 minutes, stirring occasionally until thick and pulpy. Stir in basil and cook for another 2–3 minutes. Taste and adjust seasoning. Use immediately or cool and store in the fridge for 2–3 days. Can also be frozen for up to 6 months. If you prefer a completely smooth sauce, blitz the entire batch in a blender until smooth.

NOTE: To core, peel, and chop tomatoes, remove the core from the flat end of the tomato with a sharp knife. Cut a cross on the opposite (round) end. Put tomatoes in a bowl, pour enough boiling water in to cover them, and leave for 1 minute, or until you start to see the skin lifting off. Drain and cover with cold water. Leave until cool enough to handle. Slip the skins off and roughly chop tomatoes into ½-inch pieces.

VEGETABLE STOCK MAKES APPROX. 3 QUARTS (12 CUPS)

Unlike meat-based stocks, vegetable stock is relatively quick and easy to make and will add real flavor to your soups and stews. If I'm cooking with Asian flavors, I tend to omit the thyme and bay leaf and add a couple of whole unpeeled garlic cloves, a few slices of ginger, and 1 whole long red chili—and toss in some cilantro, too. Adding button mushrooms or sliced tomatoes isn't completely unheard of either—the mushrooms add a lovely flavor and rich mouthfeel, while the tomatoes sweeten the stock.

2 tablespoons olive oil

2 large onions, unpeeled + cut into quarters

3 large carrots, unpeeled + cut into 4–5 chunks

5–6 celery stalks, cut into 4–5 chunks (leave some of the tender leaves on, too)

4 quarts (16 cups) cold water

15 whole black peppercorns

6 parsley stalks

3 fresh or dried bay leaves

A few thyme sprigs

+ Heat the oil in a large stockpot (8–10 quart would be perfect here) over medium heat. Add onion and cook, stirring often, for 2–3 minutes until starting to soften. Add carrot and celery and cook for another 6–7 minutes. I like to get a little color into my vegetables for depth of flavor and sweetness, but for light-colored stock (perhaps for risotto) just soften the vegetables without browning. Pour in 4 quarts (16 cups) cold water and add peppercorns, parsley stalks, bay leaves, and fresh thyme, bring to a boil, reduce heat to a gentle simmer, and cook for 45 minutes.

+ Remove from heat, season to taste with sea salt, and set aside until cool enough to handle. Strain stock through a fine sieve set over another large saucepan or bowl. Use immediately or store in the fridge for 2–3 days. Stock can also be frozen for 3–4 months, in which case I tend to divide and freeze in 2 cup or 1 quart plastic containers.

GLUTEN-FREE SOURDOUGH STARTER

Yes, gluten-free sourdough bread-making sounds scary—it took years for me to make my own, and I'm a chef! I understand your trepidation, but now, I've started down the sourdough path I really don't know what all the fuss was about. You do have to track down some water or milk kefir, and you do have to make this starter first, which takes a few days. However, after that, making the bread dough takes less than 10 minutes. I find it's best to begin the starter at night, just before bed, and that's how I've worded the method below. Once your starter's full of life and bubbling away, if it's looked after correctly and fed regularly, it can live for hundreds of years. Now that's a cool thought!

day one

+ Whisk ½ cup (70 g) fine brown rice flour and 1 tablespoon brewed water kefir (milk kefir works too, if that's what you've got) with ½ cup (125 ml) cold water until smooth. Transfer to a latch-top glass jar (at least 1 quart), seal, and leave in the warmest place in your house for 8–12 hours. I like to wrap the jar in a towel to keep in the warmth, and in winter you could keep it near a radiator or wrap it in a towel next to a hot water bottle.

day two (the following morning)

+ There should be visible signs of fermentation by now: there will be a distinct alcohol-like smell when you open the jar, some liquid may have risen to the top, and the bottom layer will be spongy and thick. At this stage, close the lid again and pop it into the fridge for the rest of the day.

+ Just before you go to bed that night, discard half of the starter and then add ½ cup (70 g) fine brown rice flour and ½ cup (125 ml) water. Whisk until smooth, seal jar and leave in the warmest spot in your house for 8–12 hours.

day three (the following morning)

+ The activity will have increased since yesterday. You might see a layer of liquid on the top, and you will find a thick, slightly spongy layer settled on the bottom. Keep it sealed and pop it into the fridge for the day. Just before you go to bed that night, discard half of the starter and then add 1½ cups (210 g) fine brown rice flour, 1¾ cups (375 ml) cold water, and ½ cup (50 g) ground golden flaxseeds. Whisk until smooth, transfer to a larger sealed jar (1.5–2 quarts), and leave in the warmest spot in your house for 8–12 hours.

day four (the following morning)

+ This morning you will be greeted by a lovely, thick, bubbly, active sourdough starter and you are ready to make bread. If you don't have time to make bread first thing, pop the sourdough starter into the fridge until you are ready. You will need 2 cups of starter for your loaf.

and, for the rest of your life . . .

+ Keep your starter in the fridge when you're not using it, or it will overferment and lose all its rising powers. If I'm planning to make a loaf that day, I take the starter out of the fridge first thing in the morning to bring it back to room temperature before using. But it can also be used straight from the fridge.

+ After every loaf of bread baked you need to feed your starter to keep it alive. Do this by whisking in 1¼ cups + 1 teaspoon (180 g) fine brown rice flour, 1⅔ cups (400 ml) water, and ½ cup (50 g) ground golden flaxseeds. Whisk until smooth, seal the jar, and place immediately in the fridge; no need to ferment any further on the counter.

+ To keep your starter healthy it's best to bake at least one loaf of bread a week, but you can bake every day as long as you feed your starter afterward.

+ Once you've been using and feeding the sourdough starter for a month and it's very active and strong, you can begin giving it a half feed instead of a full feed every now and then if you find you have excess starter.

+ If your starter's ever looking sad, simply add another tablespoon of water kefir to liven it up.

BROWN RICE, MILLET + CHIA SOURDOUGH BREAD MAKES 1 LOAF

Because I add psyllium husks to improve the texture of the bread and absorb extra moisture, it's hard to get good color on the top of the loaf without brushing with olive oil, so don't skip this step. At the end of the recipe you'll find a few important notes I have learned over the years about making gluten-free sourdough.

2 tablespoons chia seeds, ground or whole

6 tablespoons (90 ml) cold water

2 cups (430 g) active sourdough starter (page 238)

1 tablespoon apple cider vinegar

2 teaspoons unrefined raw sugar

1 teaspoon fine sea salt

¾ cup (100 g) millet flour or fine brown rice flour

⅔ cup (100 g) potato flour

¼ cup (60 ml) water

1 tablespoon psyllium husks

Extra-virgin olive oil, for brushing

Pumpkin, sesame, or sunflower seeds, to sprinkle, optional

+ Grease and line a small deep bread pan (the one I use is 8 x 4 x 3-inches) with parchment paper to extend up and over each side by at least 1 inch. This bread has a tendency to stick like glue, so don't skimp!

+ Combine chia seeds with 6 tablespoons (90 ml) cold water and set aside until gelled up, stirring often to prevent clumping together. Ground chia seeds will only take a few seconds to gel up; whole seeds will take around 5 minutes.

+ Whisk together sourdough starter, chia gel, cider vinegar, sugar, and salt until evenly combined. Sift in millet and potato flour and whisk well. Add ¼ cup (60 ml) water, or more if you are finding it too hard to whisk. You should be aiming for a thick batter that is still soft enough to whisk by hand, but thick enough that it isn't easy going! Think thick batter, not dough.

+ Whisk in the psyllium husks, and see it thicken up slightly when they're added. Set aside for 5 minutes before transferring mixture to the pan. Smooth the top, brush generously with olive oil, and sprinkle with seeds, if using. Place into a large (5 quart) lidded plastic container, snap on the lid, and set aside to proof for 3–8 hours. In cooler weather I mix up my bread in the morning and leave it to proof for the whole day, baking it late afternoon/ early evening.

+ When the dough is just over the top of the pan, preheat oven to 400°F (200°C). Bake bread for 10 minutes, then reduce heat to 350°F (180°C) and cook for another hour. Remove from the oven and set aside for 10 minutes before transferring to a wire rack to cool completely. (I often remove the bread from the tin and then put it back into the cooling oven and leave it there overnight.) Always leave the bread until completely cool before slicing with a sharp serrated knife for best results. Store in a plastic bag in the fridge for up to 1 week. Best toasted before eating after the first day. To freeze, slice first before placing into a plastic bag.

tips on making gluten-free sourdough

- Use golden flaxseeds instead of the more common brown ones. They absorb much more moisture and result in a high loaf with a great not-too-hard crust and mellow flavor. You can find them at health-food stores and also at selected supermarkets. Buy ground or grind your own in a blender or coffee grinder.
- Let go of how you think a bread dough should look. Gluten-free sourdough is nothing like wheat bread and should be more of a batter than a dough.
- Buy yourself a proper deep bread pan; a regular loaf tin will result in small flat bread. A 5-quart lidded plastic container is also a good investment and ensures that during the proofing stage the top of the bread doesn't dry out.
- Use digital scales to weigh everything when making bread.

FLATBREADS MAKES 4

These are superfast to prepare, even faster if you plan ahead and cook the potato ahead of time, and are perfect for scooping up spicy dhal (page 150) or wrapping around buckwheat tabouli and sprouted chickpea falafel (page 146) for an all-out feast. (When I'm making these to use as wraps, I double the recipe quantities and then divide into six larger breads that are better suited to fill and roll.) It might take you a couple of attempts to master the transferring of the sticky dough to the hot pan, but hang in there and remember that "practice makes perfect."

1 large potato, peeled and
  cut into quarters
½ cup (70 g) fine brown
  rice flour + extra, to
  dust
½ cup (55 g) chickpea
  (chana or besan) flour
¼ cup (25 g) tapioca flour
½ teaspoon gluten-free
  baking powder
¼ teaspoon baking soda
1 teaspoon psyllium husks
¼ cup (60 ml) natural
  plain yogurt
2 tablespoons warm water
Olive oil or ghee

+ Boil potato in a small saucepan of salted water for 10 minutes or until tender, drain, and then mash well. You should have about ¾ cup of mashed potato. You can use the warm mash immediately, or do in advance and keep refrigerated for later.

+ Sift brown rice, chickpea and tapioca flours, baking powder, and baking soda into a bowl, add psyllium and a good pinch of salt, and whisk to combine and evenly distribute. Add yogurt, mashed potato, and 2 tablespoons warm water and mix to form a soft dough. I usually get rid of the spoon and use my hands at this stage. The dough will form a ball and should remain slightly sticky—don't be tempted to add more flour or you run the risk of it being dry and cracking when cooked. Leave in the bowl, cover with a tea towel, and set aside for 5 minutes.

+ Heat a heavy-bottomed frying pan (cast iron is perfect) over high heat. Add a touch of oil or ghee to the pan, then using a paper towel wipe out excess and leave a light film over the base. Meanwhile, divide dough into four even pieces and roll each one into a ball. Place a sheet of parchment paper on the counter, lightly dust with extra brown rice flour, place one ball of dough on the paper, dust with a little more flour, and roll out to about ⅛-inch thick.

+ When the pan is screaming hot, quickly transfer rolled dough to the pan (I flip the rolled dough with paper still attached over onto my floured hand or onto the floured countertop and then peel back the paper before quickly and carefully transferring to the pan). Cook on both sides for 1–2 minutes until puffed and golden in patches. You may need to flip the flatbread a couple of times to brown evenly. When you've flipped the flatbread over once, you can press down on the dough with a ghee/oil-smeared paper towel to encourage it to puff up. Remove from the pan and brush with a little extra olive oil or ghee if desired. Wipe out pan with a clean paper towel and lightly grease again. Repeat with remaining dough until all four are cooked. Serve immediately.

MUCH LOVE . . .

To my babies Ada + Kye. You have changed my life beyond belief, and I can honestly say that if it weren't for you both I wouldn't be living my dream right now. It makes me so proud to see that you both share in my love of food, thank you for being honest little food critics and for allowing me to photograph you even when you were totally over it! Mama loves you both so, so much.

To Si, thank you for trusting me with this dream and encouraging me to share my recipes and stories. Thank you for looking after the kids as often as you could so I could cook and for your never-ending talent at finding props! You are the hardest working man I know, and I thank you for all that you do to give our little family the life we have. I love you always.

To Mum + Dad, you are both my biggest inspirations, and I can't ever thank you enough for the life you have given me. Thank you for holding strong to your beliefs in a world where doing so was never the easy option.

To Jessie, Ben, Louie, Vania, Gene, Mila, and Jaia, we're a mad bunch us lot, but I love you all to bits. It's been hard being so far away from you all while writing this book, and I miss you all beyond belief. Special thank you to Louie also for the hours spent proofreading both on my blog and for this book! Lotsa love to the whole Nguyen tribe, especially to Ngot for sharing your stories and wonderful food with me.

To Janna, for sharing my love of cooking and cookbooks with me from day one. To Grace, for giving me the nudge to start my blog and for your constant support and love. To Kerry and Cimmie for taking me under your wings when I felt completely lost in this new land. A special thank you to Kerry also for never taking no for an answer. I'm not sure I would have made my deadline had it not been for all the days you insisted on taking the kids so I could work! You're the best, love.

To the wonderful Vicki Marsdon, I am humbled by your belief in me, and I can't thank you enough for everything!

To Belinda, Finlay, Matt, and the crew at both HarperCollins NZ and Australia, a huge thank you!

Thanks Jude for letting me knick off with your tray (it features loads in this book!) and to all the Flexis, you ladies are awesome. To Kara, Rhyannon, Aidee, Amy, Jasmin, and Willa-May, even though we are now miles apart I could still hear your cheering from over the seas. I love you guys.

To Rosie, Andre, and Anna C for your encouragement from day one and also for your mad proofreading skills over the years. Thank you.

To everyone who gave my recipes the once-over, thank you for your honesty and for picking up on so many of my little mistakes! To Jacquie Talbot, Janet Kennedy, Sarah Kieffer, Grace Ngapo, Lan Pham, Kate Paterson, Sarah Reagle, Beth Kirby, Emma Gardner, Melissa McMahon, Hayley Wright, Lani Zaknich, Laurinda Illman, Khuong Tranter, Haidee Stairmand, Rachel Collins, Meagan Genovese, Carolyn Ellis, Alessandra Seiter, Rachael Annan, Rachel Barr, Kathleen Quayle, Nicola Galloway, Rebecca Wilcomes, Fay Edwards, Ann Walker, Alicia Walsh, Samantha Hillman, Christina Alexander, Wenda den Hollander, Hannah Cordes, Natasha

Selenitsch, Stephanie Kuttner, Kim Seiffert, Kate Finch, Megan Forsyth, Asha Soares, Rochelle Cassells, Jane Thompson, Courtney Brown, Ilana Faivel, Megan McCosker, Anita Milicevic, and Paula Corban. Much love.

To Mum, Louie, and DeArna, for helping me take a few of the photos that have me in them. To Gillian + Wayne, for your ever present encouragement and for letting me raid your mint for a photo shoot! To Nana, I love you so much. And last but not least the biggest thank you to the readers of my blog (www.mydarlinglemonthyme.com). Your comments, love, and support have never gone unnoticed, and I am constantly humbled by your kind words. This couldn't have happened without you.

Much love always xx ~emm

INDEX

almond
    arugula + pear salad with chive
        dressing 90
    piecrust 206
    shortbreads 110
almond milk 162
    pudding with cherry rose
        compote 202
anzac cookies 94
apple
    beet + fennel juice 56
    blackberry + hazelnut crumble
        194
    carrot + ginger muffins 98
apricot tarts with Kaffir lime sugar
    208
arugula, pear + almond salad with
    chive dressing 90
asparagus, orange + quinoa salad 86
avocado
    + cashew rice paper rolls 72
    chocolate tart 192
    + snow pea noodle salad with
        soy ginger sauce 64

baked butterbeans with tomato +
    feta 136
banana
    berry ice cream 182
    + blueberry breakfast muffins 58
    buckwheat + berry pancakes 28
    date + olive oil bread 112
    freezing 48 (NOTE)

bánh xèo (crispy pancakes) 126
bars—*see* cookies, brownies + bars
beans
    (dried), cooking from scratch
        136, 204 (NOTES)
    + sticky black rice with salted
        coconut cream 204
beets
    apple + fennel juice 56
    on buckwheat pancakes with
        horseradish yogurt 40
berry
    + banana ice cream 182
    buckwheat + banana pancakes
        28
    compote 42
black beans (dried), how to prepare
    204 (NOTE)
blackberry
    apple + hazelnut crumble 194
blueberry
    + banana breakfast muffins 58
bocconcini pizza with chili greens +
    olive salsa 144
bread
    banana, date + olive oil 112
    brown rice, millet + chia
        sourdough 240
    flatbreads 242
    sourdough starter 238
breakfast smoothie 48
brown rice
    how to cook 18

millet + chia sourdough bread 240
    salad with spice-roasted carrots,
        feta + pine nuts 84
brownies—*see* cookies, brownies +
    bars
buckwheat 18–20
    banana + berry pancakes 28
    dark chocolate + pear loaf 120
    how to cook 18
    pancakes with horseradish
        yogurt + beets 40
    tabouli 82, 146
butterbeans with tomato + feta,
    baked 136
buttercream, vanilla 108

cabbage, sweet + sour 148
cake(s)
    chai "cheesecake" with Earl Grey
        fig sauce 198
    chocolate coconut cupcakes 116
    flourless dark chocolate
        cardamom cake 210
    ginger whoopie pies 108
    peach, rosemary + yogurt cake
        100
carrot
    apple + ginger muffins 98
    cumin + red lentil soup with
        cilantro cashew pesto 78
    pickled 130
    spice-roasted 84
    tangelo + ginger juice 56

cashew
    + avocado rice paper rolls 72
    cilantro pesto 78
    tofu stir-fry with pickled carrot +
        chili 130
chai "cheesecake" with Earl Grey fig
    sauce 198
chermoula 128
cherry rose compote 202
chewy cranberry, millet + pistachio
    bars 104
chia
    brown rice + millet sourdough
        bread 240
    pudding, orange cinnamon 54
    seeds, soaking 48 (NOTE)
chickpea
    crackers with lentil tapenade 66
    crust 134
    falafel wraps with tahini yogurt +
        red onion relish 146
    pumpkin + kale stew with
        chimichurri + quinoa 138
    spice-roasted vegetables with
        millet + chermoula 128
chimichurri 138
chipotle sauce 30
chive dressing 90
chocolate
    avocado tart 192
    buckwheat + pear loaf 120
    cardamom cake, flourless 210
    coconut bites 122
    coconut cupcakes 116
    coconut ganache 116
    cream pops 186
    date bliss balls 102
    mousse tart 214
    orange + rosemary truffles 200
    raspberry + pistachio brownies
        106
    spiced hot 170
choux puffs with labneh +
    strawberry jam 118
cilantro cashew pesto 78
citrus dressing 86
coconut
    chocolate cupcakes 116
    cream, salted 204
    cream, whipped 22, 196, 210
    dark chocolate bites 122

    + mango jelly 212
    tahini + orange toasted muesli 36
compote
    berry-bay 42
    cherry rose 202
    strawberry lemon thyme 206
cookies, brownies + bars
    cranberry, millet + pistachio bars
        104
    ginger whoopie pies 108
    lemon, honey + thyme curd
        shortbreads 110
    quinoa + lemon anzac cookies 94
    raspberry, dark chocolate +
        pistachio brownies 106
corn
    + basil fritters 62
    cilantro + feta muffins 76
crackers, chickpea 66
cranberry, millet + pistachio bars
    104
crepes (quinoa) with orange maple
    sauce 32
crispy pancakes 126
crumble, blackberry, apple +
    hazelnut 194
cupcakes, chocolate coconut 116
curry, tofu with chili + tamarind 140

dairy alternatives 21–23, 162, 164
dandelion tea, iced 174
dark chocolate—see chocolate
date, 16
    banana + olive oil bread 112
    + chocolate bliss balls 102
    spiced pumpkin + quinoa
        muffins 114
dhal (red lentil) 150
dressings + sauces (savory)
    chipotle sauce 30
    chive dressing 90
    cilantro cashew pesto 78
    citrus dressing 86
    hoisin dipping sauce 72
    honey mustard miso dressing 80
    horseradish yogurt 40
    hot + sour sauce 72
    lemon dressing 84
    olive salsa 144
    pomegranate dressing 88
    satay sauce 68

    soy ginger dressing 64
    tahini yogurt 146
    tomato + basil sauce 234
dressings + sauces (sweet)
    Earl Grey fig sauce 198
    orange maple sauce 32
    orange yogurt 46

Earl Grey fig sauce 198
eggplant, tomato + feta salad with
    pomegranate dressing 88
eggs, poached 44
eggy baked tortilla cups 52

falafel wraps, chickpea, with tahini
    yogurt + red onion relish 146
fats + oils 16–17
fennel, beet + apple juice 56
feta
    baked butterbeans with tomato +
        136
    corn + cilantro muffins 76
    eggplant + tomato salad with
        pomegranate dressing 88
    + harissa squash galette 152
    quinoa + spinach stuffed peppers
        158
fig sauce 198
flatbreads 146, 150, 242
flaxseed, millet porridge with
    orange prunes 34
flourless dark chocolate cardamom
    cake 210
flours, gluten-free 11–15
fried Asian shallots, how to make
    64 (NOTE)
fritters, sweetcorn + basil 62
furikake 232

galette, harissa squash + feta 152
ganache, chocolate coconut 116
ghee, how to make 16–17
ginger
    carrot + apple muffins 98
    carrot + tangelo juice 56
    juice, how to make 176 (NOTE)
    kefir water 172
    nectar 176
    soy dressing 64
    whoopie pies 108
gluten-free flours 11–15

gluten-free sourdough starter 238
golden pavlova with whipped coconut cream + mango 196
green juice 56
green smoothie 50

harissa 230
  squash + feta galette 152
hazelnut, blackberry + apple crumble 194
hoisin dipping sauce 72
hokey pokey ice cream 184
honey 16
  labneh 206
  mustard miso dressing 80
horseradish yogurt 40
hot + sour sauce 72
hot chocolate, spiced 170

ice cream
  banana berry 182
  hokey pokey 184
iced dandelion tea 174
icepops
  chocolate cream 186
  watermelon, rose water + mint 178

jam, strawberry thyme 228
jars, how to sterilize for jam 228 (NOTE)
jelly, mango + coconut 212
juice
  beet, apple + fennel 56
  ginger 176 (NOTE)
  green 56
  tangelo, carrot + ginger 56

kale
  chickpea + pumpkin stew with chimichurri + quinoa 138
  latkes + sweet potato with poached eggs 44
  slaw with honey mustard miso dressing 80
kefir 24
  water, ginger 172

labneh 46, 118, 222
  honey 206

lassi, plum 166
latkes (sweet potato + kale) with poached eggs 44
lemon
  dressing 84
  honey + thyme curd shortbreads 110
lemon balm + peppermint tea 168
lentils
  (Puy-style) spaghetti 154
  (Puy-style) with sweet + sour cabbage + parsley salad 148
  (Puy-style) tapenade with chickpea crackers 66
  (red) carrot + cumin soup with cilantro cashew pesto 78
  (red) dhal 150
lime + mango slushie 188
loaf, buckwheat, dark chocolate + pear 120

mango
  + coconut jelly 212
  lime slushie 188
  + pavlova 196
milk alternatives 22–23
  almond milk 162
  walnut + maple milk 164
millet 20
  with berry-bay compote 42
  brown rice + chia sourdough bread 240
  cranberry + pistachio bars 104
  + flaxseed porridge with orange prunes 34
  how to cook 20
  spice-roasted vegetables with chickpeas + chermoula 128
muesli, tahini, orange + coconut toasted 36
muffins
  blueberry + banana 58
  carrot, apple + ginger 98
  corn, cilantro + feta 76
  spiced pumpkin, date + quinoa 114
mung bean pancakes with satay vegetables 68

noodle soup, tofu 156
noodles (rice), snow pea + avocado

salad with soy ginger dressing 64
nut
  milks 23, 162, 164
  porridge 38
nuts, how to toast 20–21

oils + fats 16–17
olive salsa 144
orange
  chocolate + rosemary truffles 200
  cinnamon + chia pudding 54
  maple sauce 32
  prunes 34
  quinoa + asparagus salad 86
  segmenting 32 (NOTE)
  tahini + coconut toasted muesli 36
  yogurt 46

pancakes
  bánh xèo (crispy) 126
  buckwheat, banana + berry 28
  buckwheat with horseradish yogurt + beets 40
  mung bean with satay vegetables 68
parsley salad 148
pavlova with whipped coconut cream + mango 196
peach, rosemary + yogurt cake 100
peanut brown rice patties 132
pear
  arugula + almond salad with chive dressing 90
  dark chocolate + buckwheat loaf 120
  how to puree 120 (NOTE)
pecan maple tart 216
peppermint + lemon balm tea 168
peppers stuffed with quinoa, spinach + feta 158
pesto, cilantro cashew 78
pickled carrot 130
piecrust
  almond 206
  chickpea 134
  savory 224
  sweet 226
  tips for making 224 (NOTE)

pistachio
   cranberry + millet bars 104
   raspberry + dark chocolate
      brownies 106
pizza
   with chili greens, bocconcini +
      olive salsa 144
   crust 144
plum lassi 166
poached eggs with squash + kale
   latkes 44
pomegranate dressing 88
popcorn, salted caramel 96
porridge
   millet + flaxseed, with orange
      prunes 34
   nut 38
prunes, orange 34
pudding
   almond milk, with cherry rose
      compote 202
   orange cinnamon chia 54
pumpkin
   chickpea + kale stew with
      chimichurri + quinoa 138
   date + quinoa muffins 114
   puree, making 114 (NOTE)
Puy-style lentils
   spaghetti 154
   with sweet + sour cabbage +
      parsley salad 148
   tapenade with chickpea crackers
      66

quiche 134
quinoa 20, 138
   crepes with orange maple sauce
      32
   how to cook 20
   + lemon anzac cookies 94
   orange + asparagus salad 86
   pumpkin + kale stew with
      chimichurri 138
   spiced pumpkin + date muffins
      114
   spinach + feta stuffed peppers
      158

raspberry, dark chocolate +
   pistachio brownies 106
red lentils

carrot + cumin soup with
   cilantro cashew pesto 78
dhal 150
red onion relish 146
rhubarb with orange yogurt 46
rice 17–18
   how to cook 18
   millet + chia sourdough bread
      240
   patties, peanut 132
   salad with spice-roasted carrots,
      feta + pine nuts 84
   sticky black, + beans with salted
      coconut cream 204
rice paper rolls with avocado +
   cashew 72
roasted cherry tomato quiche with
   chickpea crust 134
roasted rhubarb with orange
   yogurt 46
roasted squash, sweet potato +
   cilantro soup 70

salad
   arugula, pear + almond with
      chive dressing 90
   brown rice with spice-roasted
      carrots, feta + pine nuts 84
   buckwheat tabouli 82
   eggplant, tomato + feta with
      pomegranate dressing 88
   kale slaw with honey mustard
      miso dressing 80
   noodle (rice), snow pea +
      avocado with soy ginger
      dressing 64
   orange, quinoa + asparagus 86
   parsley 148
   rice with spice-roasted carrots,
      feta + pine nuts 84
salsa, olive 144
salted caramel popcorn 96
salted coconut cream 204
satay
   sauce 68
   vegetables with mung bean
      pancakes 68
sauces—see dressings + sauces
savory piecrust, 152, 224
seeds, how to toast 20–21
segmenting an orange 32 (NOTE)

shallots (Asian), how to fry 64 (NOTE)
shortbreads
   almond 110
   lemon, honey + thyme curd 110
slaw, kale, with honey mustard
   miso dressing 80
slushie, mango lime 188
smoothie
   breakfast 48
   green 50
snow pea
   + avocado noodle salad with soy
      ginger dressing 64
   prepping 69 (NOTE)
sorbet, strawberry + Thai basil 180
soup
   carrot, cumin + red lentil with
      cilantro cashew pesto 78
   roasted squash, sweet potato +
      cilantro70
   tofu noodle 156
sourdough
   bread 240
   starter 238, 240
soy ginger dressing 64
spaghetti, lentil 154
spice roasted vegetables with
   chickpeas, millet + chermoula
   128
spiced hot chocolate 170
spiced pumpkin, date + quinoa
   muffins 114
spices, how to toast 20–21
spinach, quinoa + feta stuffed
   peppers 158
squash
   + feta galette 152
   sweet potato + cilantro soup 70
sterilizing jars for jam 228 (NOTE)
stew, chickpea, pumpkin + kale,
   with chimichurri + quinoa
   138
sticky black rice + beans with salted
   coconut cream 204
stock
   for tofu noodle soup 156
   vegetable 236
strawberry
   lemon thyme compote 206
   lemon thyme tarts with honey
      labneh 206

+ thai basil sorbet 180
thyme jam 118, 228
stuffed peppers with quinoa,
    spinach + feta 158
sweet + sour cabbage 148
sweet + sour lemongrass tempeh
    142
sweet piecrust 226
sweet potato
    + kale latkes with poached eggs
    44
    roasted squash + cilantro soup
    70
sweetcorn
    + basil fritters 62
    cilantro + feta muffins 76
sweeteners 15–16

tabouli, buckwheat 82
tahini 24
    orange + coconut toasted muesli
    36
    yogurt 146
tamarind puree, how to make 140
    (NOTE)
tangelo, carrot + ginger juice 56
tapenade, lentil, with chickpea
    crackers 66
tart(s)

apricot with Kaffir lime sugar
    208
chocolate avocado 192
chocolate mousse 214
harissa squash + feta galette 152
pecan maple 216
strawberry lemon thyme with
    honey labneh 206
tea
    iced dandelion 174
    peppermint + lemon balm 168
tempeh, sweet + sour lemongrass
    142
toasting spices, seeds + nuts 20–21
tofu
    curry with chili + tamarind 140
    noodle soup 156
    scramble with chipotle sauce 30
    stir-fry with pickled carrot,
        cashew + chili 130
tomato
    baked butterbeans with feta +
        136
    + basil sauce 136, 144, 154, 234
    eggplant + feta salad with
        pomegranate dressing 88
    how to peel 234 (NOTE)
    quiche with chickpea crust 134
tortilla cups, eggy baked 52

truffles, dark chocolate, orange +
    rosemary 200

vanilla buttercream 108
vegetable stock 70, 78, 236
vegetables (spice roasted)
    with chickpeas, millet +
    chermoula 128

walnut + maple milk 164
warm lentils with sweet + sour
    cabbage + parsley salad 148
warm millet with berry-bay
    compote 42
watermelon, rose water + mint
    icepops 178
white rice, how to cook 18
whoopie pies, ginger 108
wraps with chickpea falafel,
    tahini yogurt + red onion
    relish 146

yogurt
    peach + rosemary cake 100
    horseradish 40
    how to make 220
    labneh 222
    orange 46
    tahini 146

ABOUT THE AUTHOR

Emma Galloway is a New Zealand–born chef now living in Perth, Australia. A mother of two, she writes a successful food blog based on her personal food philosophy of achieving a better life through nutritious, wholesome, real cooking.

www.mydarlinglemonthyme.com